K·I·T·C·H·E·N
Antiques

FRANCES JOHNSON

Schiffer Publishing Ltd

77 Lower Valley Road, Atglen, PA 19310

Library of Congress Cataloging-in-Publication Data

Johnson, Frances.
    Kitchen antiques with values / Frances Johnson.
        p. cm.
    ISBN 0-88740-950-4 (paper)
    1. Kitchen utensils--Collectors and collecting--United States--
Catalogs. I. Title.
NK6140.J65 1996
745.1'0973'075--dc20   95-49222
                              CIP

Printed in Hong Kong
ISBN: 0-88740-950-4

Published by Schiffer Publishing Ltd.
77 Lower Valley Road
Atglen, PA 19310
Please write for a free catalog.
This book may be purchased from the publisher.
Please include $2.95 for shipping.
Try your bookstore first.

We are interested in hearing from authors
with book ideas on related subjects.

Contents

Introduction

From the era of the Colonists to that of fast food restaurants the kitchen has remained the warmest, the most cheerful room, and the one enjoyed most by the family. Actually, it was about the only room in the house large enough for the whole family to gather at once, and early on it was the only one that was warm on cold, winter nights. Maybe in those early days it wasn't as colorful, nor as inviting as we have been lead to believe. Except for the warmth and love offered by the family, it would have been a dark and dreary place. You see in those very early days the walls were unpainted and dark from the smoke from the woodburning fireplace where all the cooking was done. The windows were small and dark, and the furnishings sparse. In those early days and probably for a century or more most of the furnishings were handmade, either by the owner or by a neighbor who was more skilled yet was willing to barter with his less skilled neighbors. The rich merchants and planters were able to have their furnishings shipped from Europe or specially made by the furniture makers who have since become famous. But there were hundreds more struggling farmers and tradesmen who couldn't afford the services of those craftsmen; they had to be satisfied with whatever they or their neighbors could build.

Less than a century after the arrival of the Pilgrims the scene had changed completely except for the fireplace cooking. They still cooked over the same hearth which furnished heat during the winter, but they began adding small things to make life a little easier. One of those additions was a seat, something like the later window seats, that was built on either side of the fireplace. The seats served more than one purpose – now the children had a place to sit and study that was warm and better lit than the floor where they had formerly sat. There was a lack of chairs in those days, in fact they often used the homemade wagon seat or chairs in the kitchen during the week and in the wagon for the ride to church on Sunday. That was also a time when they had to depend on homemade candles for light. The light from the fireplace was enough for the children to read or study by and it saved candles. Still later these seats would be replaced with chimney cupboards, a much sought after antique today.

The early settlers, including those moving westward later, had to clear the fields which required a lot of work. They needed all the help they could get, and the best way to get it and keep it, they seem to think, was by having large families. That meant a new baby was born about every year. Except for the rich cotton and tobacco planters who had mammies to care for the children, the others had to be cared for by their mothers. That meant that a cradle almost became a permanent fixture in the kitchen. Those cradles, ranging from crudely hollowed-out versions to fine brightly decorated Pennsylvania Dutch examples, are very collectible today.

The parents slept in the kitchen from the very beginning, and this was out of necessity. At first it was the only room in the house except for the loft — which could only by the biggest stretch of the imagination be called a room. Young children could also be found in the kitchen at night. Since there were always several small children as well as the latest baby, a trundle bed was essential. It could be kept under the parent's bed during the day and pulled out at night so the younger children would have a place to sleep, and they too could have a warm place at night. Parents slept near the fire, replenishing the logs at night to keep the fire from going out. They had to keep the fire going as in those very early days they didn't have matches to start another one. If the fire went out, some member of the family had to go to the nearest neighbor's for live coals to start a new fire. It was easier to keep the old fire burning than freeze until new coals were brought in. As with everything else, progress was being made and it wasn't too long before families began to acquire and keep a supply of flint and steel as it had been found those two would start a new fire. No longer were hot coals necessary.

A fire was kept burning year round as all the food had to be cooked in the fireplace. Iron pots and kettles hung in or near the fire while biscuits were baked in Dutch ovens on the hearth. Later ovens were built into the side of the chimneys and they were used to bake cakes, pies, and bread. Some of the food might have been a bit simpler although they used more herbs in their cooking, but it was delicious as can be proved by the cooks who still demonstrate fireplace cooking at some of the restorations around the country. Some of these cooks are using recipes passed down from their mothers and grandmothers.

It would be a century or more before families would learn how to pump water into the house, and even longer before they actually had running water as we know it now. It would be even longer, not until around this century, that electricity would be available. In fact, many rural farm families didn't get electricity until after World War II.

This information is offered so young collectors can make a comparison between life as it was years ago and the modern conveniences we enjoy today. In fact, the original idea was to design a book that would let the readers see how the old kitchens were furnished by providing a sample of kitchen antiques and collectibles, and then let readers decide whether they want to create a replica of that old kitchen or only enhance their modern kitchen with a few choice pieces.

Modern conveniences, especially electrical appliances, did not begin to creep into the lives of our ancestors until around the beginning of the twentieth century. But once they started, electrical appliances grew by leaps and bounds. The first three quarters of this century seemed to have seen more growth than any other period, and the majority of antiques and collectibles used in this book are from that period. Judging by the many conversations we have had with both antique dealers and collectors, it seems the most desirable kitchen things are those from around 1930 to maybe 1970. A generation or so ago collectors were searching for and collecting old trestle tables, settles, sugar chests, iron cooking tools and utensils, candle molds, Betty lamps, and corner cupboards. Today there is another group of collectors, a younger group, that is much like the older group because they, too, want to collect what they remember from grandmother's house. Their grandmothers had electricity, therefore they used electrical appliances like irons, percolators, toaster, waffle irons, popcorn poppers, and mixers. Whereas earlier collectors had searched for Staffordshire, flint glass and ironstone, the younger collectors are searching for Depression glass, Fiesta ware and pottery made in several of the southern potteries.

There does not seem to be as many specialized collectors today as there were half a century ago. At that time it seemed the collector only collected in one or two categories. For example, a collector might collect pattern glass or they might collect cut glass, but seldom, if ever, did they collect the two things at one time. Then there were the china collectors, either Staffordshire or Haviland. I never knew a collector who collected both — it was always one or the other. I once knew a collector who loved the finest of Haviland, and insisted on using it daily. Since a complete set was so expensive she could not afford it, she found another solution. She enjoyed "antiquing," so went every chance she got. She would buy odd pieces in certain patterns of Haviland and eventually match up place settings, one in each pattern. She would then mix and match her china as well as place settings in each of the patterns of sterling flatware she had accumulated the same way she had bought the Haviland.

Today's collectors seem to prefer a more eclectic accumulation. They are as liable to collect glass and iron as aluminum and sterling. Actually one of the most desirable items in the kitchen category now seems to be small tools and utensils. Some collectors lean towards the tools with either red, green, yellow, or blue handles. Some even mix and match these colors; but the majority seems to prefer red. A couple of collections, all red, have been seen and they are certainly attractive. It is rather easy today to assemble an assortment of baskets, cast aluminum cookware, egg tools, and even butter molds and paddles, and display them all in one kitchen. But a word of caution: Watch those butter molds. New ones that the makers or the sellers have tried to age have been coming in from Canada for about a decade.

Of course these collections depend entirely on the whims and purse of the one collecting them. With this eclectic style of collecting, it is possible to choose only the best, both in price and condition, in each category. Whatever the reason, this seems to be a time of diversified collecting.

It is hoped the information given in this book will help new collectors by showing them some of the many things available, and the prices will help them make better choices. These prices are not intended to be carved in stone, but rather to be used as a guide. It is next to impossible to find a price that will be perfect for the same item in all parts of the country as prices vary from one location to another. Demands also vary from one location to another, and this also has a bearing on prices. Condition also has a great bearing on prices because there is no place in the country where a damaged piece will bring anything like that of a perfect piece. But by averaging prices from many areas we hope the following are fair prices in your area.

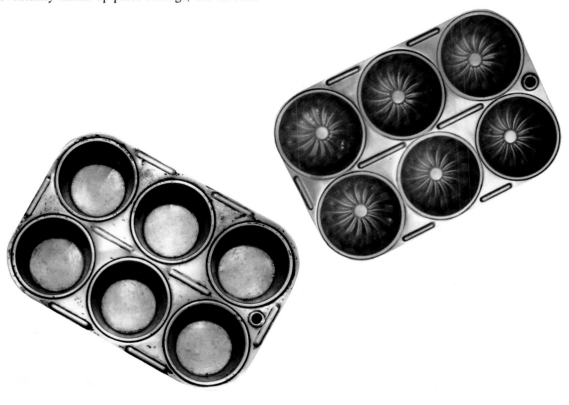

Chapter One
Aluminum, Cast and Otherwise

Chances are the Pilgrims and many who followed them brought blacksmith-made iron cooking pots. It is also quite possible that all of them soon learned how to cook various foods found in the New World using the waterproof basketry and pottery pieces made by the Indians. Iron cooking tools and utensils continued in use for years; in fact, some of them are still being used today.

Then the tinsmiths began converging on the settlers, their wagons jingling and jangling with an assortment of tinwares they had brought from their home shops. Generally in those early days the tinsmiths spent the winter making new pieces to peddle to the settlers during the spring and summer. As a tinsmith made his rounds, he would even stop long enough to make a piece to fit the housewife's needs or to repair a piece he had sold previously. Repairs were actually a big part of his business, and it was less expensive for the housewife than buying new pieces. It took years, but as new materials began to replace tin, the tinsmiths began cutting back on their territories. He was missed when a seam needed to be repaired or a new handle attached, but a little metal disk called a Mendet became available to mend the holes in both tin and graniteware, so the tinsmith wasn't missed as much as some had feared.

By the time graniteware hit the market the women were ready for a change. They welcomed the colorful graniteware and it became a success — almost overnight. Graniteware was bright, colorful, and easy to clean so they were overjoyed, but still women didn't discard their old iron pieces. Instead they packed the iron away — just in case this fancy new cookware was not satisfactory.

The next material used to make cooking utensils and tools was aluminum. It was shiny and bright, much prettier than the old iron ware, and it was even easier to clean than the graniteware. It was also easier to keep clean. Aluminum was actually a late bloomer, although it was discovered much earlier. It was not even identified until 1807 when Sir Humphrey Davy established its existence. One of the reasons for not being able to identify it sooner, they said, was the fact it was mixed with other elements to form such desirable materials as sapphires, rubies, garnets, and emeralds. With stones like that, who was looking for aluminum although when it was finally identified, it was more expensive than gold or silver. This stemmed partly from the fact that even though it had been identified, nobody had devised a way to mine it and produce pure aluminum. That meant the small amounts that finally reached the market were very expensive.

Then in 1825 a Danish scientist named Hans Christain Orsted produced a small pellet of pure aluminum, and the race was on to see who could or who would be able to mine aluminum. But it was not an easy chore, apparently, as it would be another twenty years before a German named Frederick Woehler would be able to produce pure aluminum, and then it would only be in a gray powder form. It was nearly ten years later before a French chemist named Henri St. Claire Deville was able to develop a method for producing marble-sized balls of aluminum. His method caused the price of aluminum to drop $528 a pound. The 1845 price of $545 had held steady until Deville's discovery, then it dropped to $17 a pound where it stayed until the big discovery in 1886. That was the time when an American named Charles Hall and a Frenchman named Paul Heroult, each working alone, discovered a process for producing aluminum that was both easy and inexpensive. Again the price dropped quickly, this time to $5 a pound, and by 1900 it was selling for only 33 cents a pound. That was when aluminum really hit its stride. Shortly thereafter it began to be used for making everything from pots and pans to Rolls-Royce car bodies.

Within a decade The Aluminum Cooking Utensil Company of Pittsburgh, Pennsylvania began issuing a catalog showing the many cooking utensils they offered. Their trademark was "Wear-Ever" which was meant, no doubt, to describe the durability of their products. It was, and still is, correct if we are to judge by the many pieces found today. Most of those found now are in good condition. That easily recognized trademark is a slightly elongated circle divided into four sections with a band up and down and another across. The four sections that look like slices of a pie have a star in each while the top to bottom band has the word aluminum and the cross band has T.A.C.U.Co. Their 1909, forty page catalog began with pictures, descriptions, and sizes of coffee and tea pots. Sizes ranged from one to three quarts and prices from $2 to $3 each.

Other items shown in that catalog were sauce pans, preserving kettles up to 24 quart size, pudding pans, dairy pans, cake pans, and bread pans. The choice of cake pans ranged from mountain cake which was round, to a jelly cake pan that was quite shallow, to square cake pans with solid or loose bottoms. There was also a choice of tube cake pans and turban cake molds. Muffin and corn cake pans were quite similar although the corn cake pan looked more shallow. There were oval jelly molds, baking pans, double roasters, an assortment of cups which probably explains why they are still so plentiful, and dippers. That was a time when a dipper, either tin or aluminum, hung by the well so that anybody, friend or foe, needing a drink of water was welcome to refresh himself. Early on gourds

Original sizzling steak platter, cast aluminum made by Wagner Ware, Sidney, Ohio. $25-$35

Close-up of back of platter

were cut and used as dippers in buckets of water, especially those taken to workers in the fields. But after aluminum became plentiful and inexpensive, aluminum dippers were used while gourds were discarded. Among the things in the catalog considered more luxurious, or maybe less necessary, were the griddle cake covers, chafing dishes, porringers, tea steepers, dinner pails, spice cabinets, and flasks. Those pieces were available in regular aluminum while in cast aluminum there were tea kettles, odorless cookers, covered broilers, frying pans or skillets, oyster stew pans, waffle irons, and griddles. In the griddle category there were the round ones with a side handle, round with a bail, and an oblong design. These pieces were recommended for use in the home while several pages were devoted to pieces for hotel use. Among the hotel pieces were trays in assorted sizes and shapes, sauce pans up to 100 quart capacity, coffee boilers up to 25 quart capacity, frying pans, Bain Marie pots, and two styles of self-righting cuspidors.

Wear-Ever also gave explicit instructions in the catalog for "caring" for the aluminum cookware. Unfortunately only the store owner received a copy, but if he studied it as the company expected him to, he could explain to his customers how to take care of their aluminum cookware. It is interesting now to share that information when one finds an old catalog. The catalog began by saying that the prevalent idea that aluminum utensils required no cleaning or polishing was erroneous. They went on to say that all aluminum utensils were bright and attractive, and for that reason readily showed dirt spots. "Ordinarily," they

said, "the free use of pure soap and hot water will keep them in perfect condition."

We are not recommending any of the following cleaning idea, only quoting from the 1909 catalog with the thought that if the factory recommended it, it can't be all bad, and it should work on the older pieces we are collecting. They suggested the outside polished surface be kept bright with the used of whiting or any good polish, especially polishes that were available at that time like Polishine, Solarine, or Bon Ami. Some of these may not be available today, and we are not sure which, if any, substitutes will work, however they did recommend that old and badly discolored aluminum pieces be taken to a machine shop where they could be repolished on a buffing wheel. We have tried this suggestion and found it works beautifully.

It was also suggested that the liberal used of Sapolio or Old Dutch Cleanser would help brighten aluminum that had been darkened by the use of water containing alkalies or iron. These same cleaners would help clean utensils that had burned food or grease on them. Many of the pieces found today have this problem so this suggestion should prove very helpful, and might even save some fine piece. If the food and grease was badly burned into the surface, they said, it could usually be soaked loose by keeping hot water in the utensil for several hours after which it could be removed by scraping with a wooden spoon. If this method and scouring it with the cleaners mentioned above did not work, it was time for drastic measures like scouring it with fine sand and powdered emery.

One of their suggestions for caring for aluminum cooking utensils is of special interest to collectors today who may find a choice piece in deplorable condition. "If by years of neglect or by accident a vessel is covered with burned grease and foreign matter, it can easily be cleaned by using four tablespoons of oxalic acid crystals in a gallon of water for no more than five minutes (or by allowing this solution to remain cold in the vessel overnight); then, before using, wash carefully with clean hot water and soap." It may not be possible now to get the crystals everywhere, but surely there is an equivalent that will work. If it will, it could save many fine, old pieces of aluminum cookware. The manufacturer also cautioned against using knives and other sharp instruments to scrape the utensils. Instead they suggested the use of a wooden spoon. Families didn't have plastic spoons at that time. They used their wooden ones like we use our plastic ones now — for everything. That was also a time when women made most of their own soap, and it was called lye soap. That probably explains why the company stressed the fact one should not use lye, ashes, ammonia, or any washing powder or soap containing alkalies.

Wear-Ever was not the only manufacturer of aluminum cooking utensils. Both Wagner and Griswold made a variety of aluminum as well as their famous iron wares. West Bend also made a variety of aluminum pieces, but they are not nearly as plentiful as those made by the other three companies. Then numerous pieces can be found with no mark at all indicating other companies were engaged in their manufacture. In fact, so many pieces have been seen it is enough to boggle the mind of the collector.

Another confusing fact is that pieces with no marks could pass for cast aluminum or less expensive pewter. When it is so difficult to distinguish between them, it has been found they usually blend together well. An example of this is the creamer, sugar, and syrup pitcher in the illustrations. They were believed to be cast aluminum when bought, but at home there was a question. Since they work so well with marked aluminum pieces, the question has been forgotten.

Cast aluminum Wagner Ware platter with different design. $25-$35

Cast aluminum platter with similar design. Unmarked. $20-$30

Back view of platter

West Bend cast aluminum server or platter. $35-$40

Cast aluminum syrup pitcher, unmarked. $15-$20

Cast aluminum creamer and sugar, unmarked. $25-$35 pair

Aluminum sugar sifter, unmarked. $10-$12

9

Sugar dish marked Pure Aluminum. $15-$18

Aluminum beverage set, 8 tumblers, pitcher, original tray, Buenilum trademark. $200-$250

Aluminum beverage set, pitcher and 8 tumblers in circa 1940 basketry carrier, Buenilum trademark. $175-$225 beverage set, $75-$85 carrier

Lazy Susan with original serving dishes, circa 1950s, made by West Bend Aluminum Company, 20 inches diameter. $45-$50

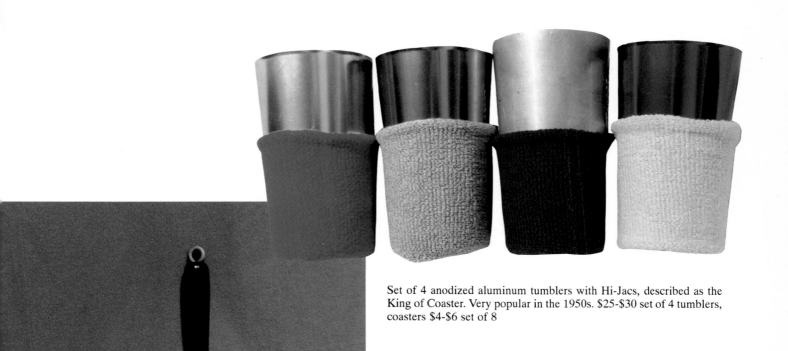

Set of 4 anodized aluminum tumblers with Hi-Jacs, described as the King of Coaster. Very popular in the 1950s. $25-$30 set of 4 tumblers, coasters $4-$6 set of 8

Cast aluminum griddle with handle. $15-$20

Cast aluminum griddle with bail, Griswold trademark. $30-$40

Aluminum pie server, unmarked. $10-$13

Cast aluminum water kettle, Griswold trademark. $50-$60

Aluminum lunch bucket with soup container on top, unmarked. $28-$32

Trademark on bottom of kettle.

Advertising ashtray shaped like a skillet. Marked Aluma-Cast Industries, Reading, Massachusetts. $12-$18

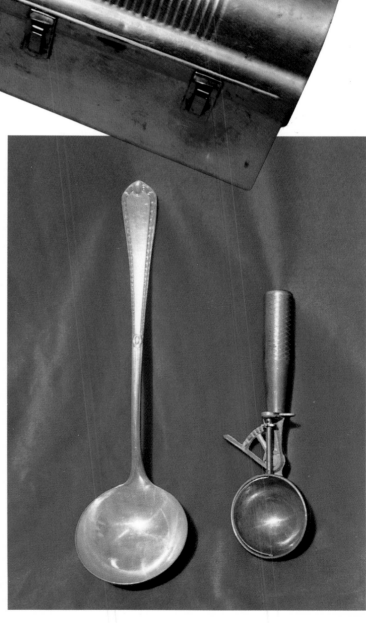

Aluminum lunch box, thermos in top, unmarked. $22-$27

Wall-hung, hand-crank aluminum fruit juicer, unmarked. $10-$15

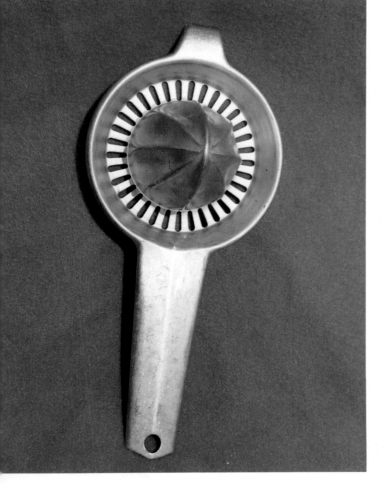

Aluminum fruit juicer, unmarked. $5-$8

Aluminum ice cream scoop, unmarked. Serving spoon marked Aluminum, Germany. Scoop $14-$19, spoon $12-$17

Aluminum funnel for filling fruit jars, unmarked. $5-$8

Aluminum bar tool, trade name Bar-boy, bottle opener and jigger measure. $7-$9

Aluminum canape molds, unmarked. $13-$18

Spun aluminum ice bucket with black band. $10-$15

Oval aluminum jelly mold, priced $1.60 in Wear-Ever's (The Aluminum Cooking Utensil Company) 1909 catalogue. $17-$23

Large, heavy cast aluminum pitcher, unmarked. $20-$25

Heavy aluminum fork, 9 inches long, made by Friendly Fork Company, Dayton, Ohio. $17-$22

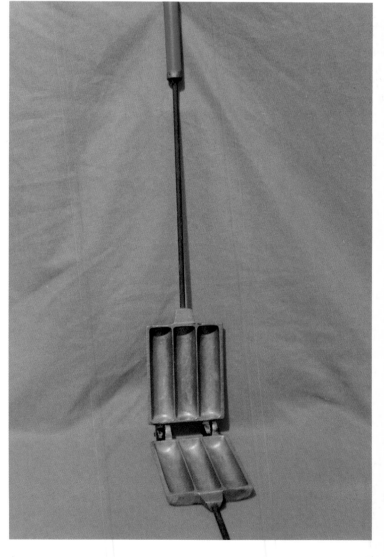

Long handled hot dog toaster, cast aluminum. $25-$30

Hot Dog Toastee closed.

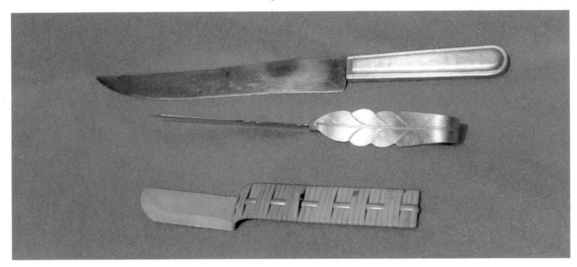

Three aluminum knives. Bamboo wrapped handle $9-$12, knife in middle $15-$18, long knife $7-$9

Late cast aluminum griddle. $12-$15

16

Chapter Two
Baking, Boiling, and Brewing

Once man devised tools and utensils for use in the cooking process, the same shapes, sizes, and materials were used for centuries. This is based on the theory that records show the Roman kitchens of the first century had a few of the utensils we still enjoy like copper sauce pans, kettles, colanders, and believe it or not, egg poachers. We still use those things today along with one of the original tools used by the cavemen, the spit. Today the spit is more sophisticated, it is called a rotisserie, and it is often found on the outside grill. This is additional proof that the more things change, the more they stay the same.

Methods of cooking didn't change a heck of a lot from those early Romans to the first settlers in the New World who built log cabins and cooked over the fire in the fireplace. Later they would build ovens on the side of the fireplaces for baking. Then they began to acquire woodburning stoves for cooking. The stoves, along with the servants, soon became fixtures in the south, where many of the first settlers who came from rich European families began making money here. This money came from the cotton and tobacco they grew and sent back to their homeland to be sold. It was the custom in the south to build the kitchen away from the main part of the house. Now the masses didn't build their kitchens away from their log cabins, only the rich planters and merchants with large, expensive homes. Building the kitchens away from the main part of the house, especially the dining room, was an effort to not only keep the odors away but was also an effort to keep the heat from the cooking away from the main house as it did and still does get extremely hot and humid in the south. Servants carried the food from the kitchen to the dining room which could be a distance of several hundred feet, in some instances. Some concerned homeowners built a sort of covered walkway from the kitchen to the dining room so the food, hopefully, would not got get wet in case of rain, nor get too cold.

Then came the Industrial Revolution when everybody tried to make a better mouse trap. In the case of kitchenware, everybody got into the act, trying to build a labor saving device or a utensil that was more useful or easier to use. Once started, the trend has continued until today — when new things come on the market almost daily. The old basic pots and pans haven't changed that much, rather it is the material used to make them that has changed so much. Whereas the farm wife once anxiously awaited the arrival of the tinsmith to get new utensils, now the utensils of choice are teflon lined and many are produced from glass-like materials. Of course there are many new things, things to make the work easier like dishwashers, blenders, and all electrical appliances. Most of us like to collect a few things from the early years (especially the handmade tools some ingenious husband made for this wife to make her work easier) but today most collectors are interested in kitchenware from around 1930 through 1960. There are several reasons for this, with perhaps the most important being the fact these later things are easier to find. They are also less expensive, and the majority of the younger collectors remember their mothers using them.

Iron utensils are still available in stores, and some of the Griswold pieces are being reproduced. Wagner has never stopped production as far as is known. Tin and aluminum pieces are still being made, but often the older ones can be found at cheaper prices. Fire King and Pyrex prices vary from one place to another. In yard sales they can be bought for a song, but in antique shops and malls the prices can be quite high.

As we have pointed out before, there were not that many restaurants before World War II, especially in small towns and rural areas. Even in the cities there was lots of home entertaining and it was encouraged by the many women's magazines on the market at that time. Each hostess wanted to entertain as graciously as, or maybe better than, the other ladies in her circle, and the manufacturers were more than anxious to help by supplying the newest and best tools, utensils, and gadgets. One of those that might pass as a gadget was the canape mold. These molds were made by different companies, distributed under different trade names, and had different designs. One has been found in the original box. This one was sold under the trade name of Pettee Pattees. It consists of four molds that can be attached to four prongs on a long handle. Although no patent date is shown, it appears to date around 1940.

It is always great to find the box in which anything was packaged, especially in the collectibles field, but in this case it was even nicer as instructions on an item's use (as well as a recipe) are printed on the lid. Probably the most important information on the box lid is a picture of the filled molds, and a list of the foods that can be used to fill them. Among the specialized foods are caviar, anchovy paste, chopped chicken liver, creamed salmon, and a variety of cheeses. Then the manufacturer suggested one might like sardine paste, a number of combinations using seafoods, meats, and vegetables. Seems anything could be used in the molds, but first the mold had to be assembled. Instructions were given for this chore as well as a recipe for the batter in which the mold had to be dipped before it could be cooked in hot oil — never over 370 degrees nor under 350.

Tin, tube cake pan. $9-$11

In case there is a collector without a recipe but who would like to use their canape molds, the following was given with this set. Only four ingredients were needed: one cup flour, one cup milk, one egg, and a half teaspoon of salt. These ingredients should be mixed thoroughly to about the consistency of heavy cream. They stressed the fact that no baking powder or yeast was to be used. After dipping the molds into the hot oil, they were then dipped, just to the top of the molds, in the batter mixture. They were then put back into the hot oil where they were left for a few seconds or until the mold turned golden brown. This recipe was sufficient to make one hundred shells, about twenty five in each shape, they said.

The wafering iron is another tool that has experienced a long and useful career. First made in the 19th century, wafering irons have continued to be used, either the older ones or those made more recently. This is another item for which most of the original recipes have been lost. One has been found in an 1896 magazine. It was described as perfect for making wafers or Swiss bratselinni, the Swiss name for wafers. In case other collectors are looking for a recipe to use with their irons, this one worked perfectly for us. "Mix until creamy one cup sweet butter and one cup sugar. Add two well beaten eggs, one teaspoon powdered cinnamon, and enough flour to make a batter that can be formed into small balls about the size of a large marble. Place the balls of dough on a hot, buttered wafer iron, close the iron and hold it for a few minutes in or directly over the fire — just long enough for it to brown the wafer delicately." (Remember in 1896 lots of people were still cooking on fireplaces and woodburning cookstoves which furnished an open fire when the eye of the stove had been removed. Today they work better on a gas stove than an electric.) It was also found that the wafers were more tasty if they were carefully curled around a hot stick or the equivalent while still hot.

Early baking led to the need for other pieces. No longer was a simple pan sufficient. As the Industrial Revolution continued, all types of cake pans, both tube and bundt, cookie cut-

ters, baking sheets were made. With all these cookies being baked, another need arose. Homemakers needed a cookie jar in which to store all the cookies.

Pie birds are about as old as most of the ceramic items made for use in the kitchen, but like so many things their popularity waned as more bakeries offered ready made pies. They are bird-shaped porcelain pieces with open mouths and bases that are still used, although sparingly now that so many women are working outside the home today. They simply don't have time to bake pies as they once did, so the pie birds have been relegated to the attic or basement along with so many things from earlier eras.

The pie bird in the illustration is a later one, probably dating around 1950. Again the box was found with it and it is described as a Yankee Pie Bird, for no other reason it seems than the fact it was made in New Hampshire. According to the instructions it is place on the bottom crust, then the filling is poured in, and the top crust put on. Naturally a hole has to be made to slip the crust over the bird. This is fine except the hole will have to be patched so it fits snugly around the bird. Once the pie starts to cook, the steam will escape through the bird's beak, and the juices will boil up into the body of the pie bird. This keeps it from cooking over the top crust. The maker suggested the bird be left in the pie until after the first few slices are removed as it gives the pie a party look.

The reason for having a tea kettle in this category, albeit an electric one, is the fact that almost since time immemorial there has always been a kettle of hot water in every kitchen. The hot water might be used to make a cup of tea or coffee, or simply to add to food about to boil dry. Whatever the reason, the kettle was usually on the fire or on the stove.

From the very early days the housewife saved as much of summer's bounty as possible. She made apple juice and cider which she canned along with the tomato and grape juice. Imagine her joy when the bottle capper became available. She was able to bottle the juices and put a snug cap on them, one that would usually preserve the juices until she was ready to serve them. The bottle capper was used for yet another chore during the Prohibition period of the Twenties. Many men made bathtub gin or home brew that had to be bottled and capped.

Potato masher, could be used for any root vegetable. $8-$12

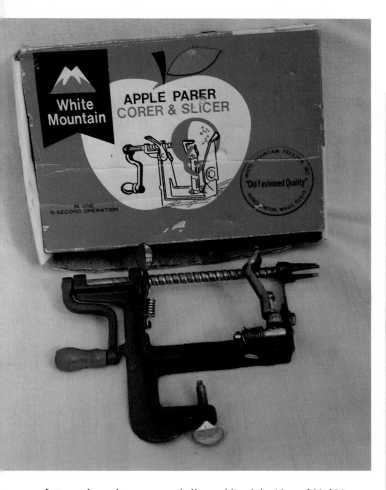

Late apple peeler, corer, and slicer with original box. $23-$30

Pyrex well and tree platter, popular in the 1950s. $18-$23

Inexpensive little cook books, actually booklets, are again gaining popularity. Can be found in most flea markets and malls. $1-$2 each depending on content and condition

19

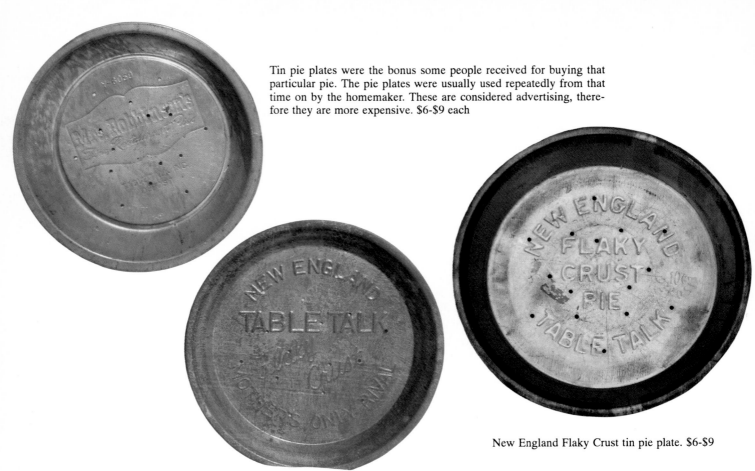

Tin pie plates were the bonus some people received for buying that particular pie. The pie plates were usually used repeatedly from that time on by the homemaker. These are considered advertising, therefore they are more expensive. $6-$9 each

New England Flaky Crust tin pie plate. $6-$9

Old iron pan bakes a dozen rolls at once. $24-$32

Handmade, wooden cutting board. $25-$28

Tin, brown bread pan, lid missing.
$20-$25, with lid $30-$40

Aluminum cookie cutters with Christmas designs. $10-$12

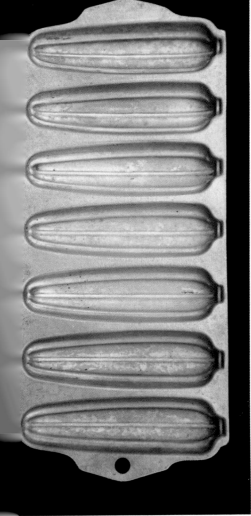

Aluminum corn stick pan, Wear-Ever
trademark. $15-$19

Muffin or cup cake pan, bakes a dozen, late. $7-$9

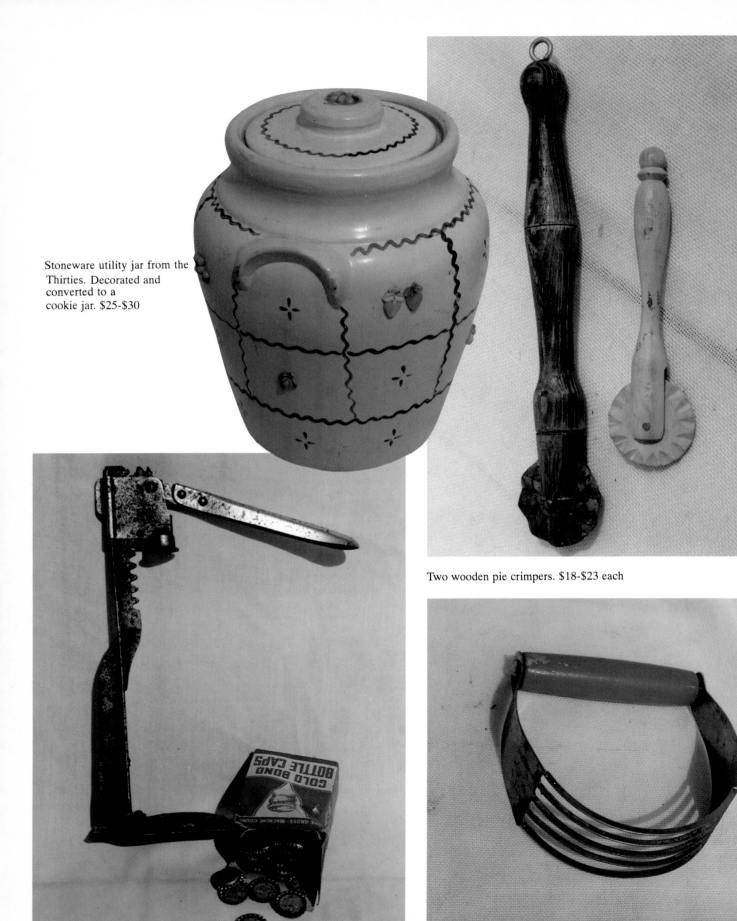

Stoneware utility jar from the Thirties. Decorated and converted to a cookie jar. $25-$30

Two wooden pie crimpers. $18-$23 each

Fruit juices and wines were bottled to save for winter. The bottle capper was an essential tool for this chore. $15-$20

Pastry blender with much sought after red handle. $8-$10

Two medium-sized, iron bean pots. Older ones were used for cooking in the fireplace. $16-$22

Pettee Pattee canape molds assembled.

Pettee Pattee canape molds in original box.

The original owner used these to decorate cakes. They were stuck into the cake, filled with frosting, and a candle or flower was inserted. They were new in 1954. $18-$24

Cookie cutters consisting of a Christmas tree, candy cane, and two stars. $8-$10

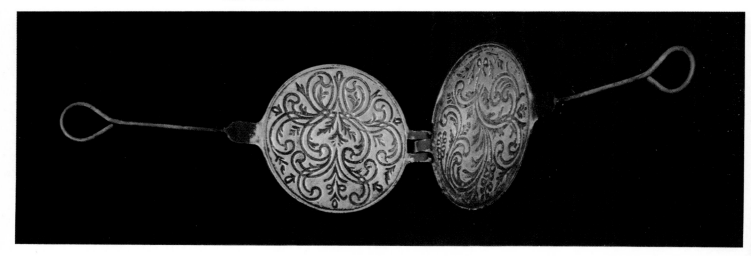

Late wafering irons. $35-$40

24

Two aluminum muffin pans in different shapes. $5-$7 each

Three Fire King soup bowls. Circa 1950. $8-$10 each

Half a set of Pyrex mixing bowls. $22-$30 for a complete set

Iron popover pan, bakes eleven. $22-$30

Large stoneware bean pot. Often used now to hold tools on the kitchen counter. $30-$35 without lid, $35-$45 with lid

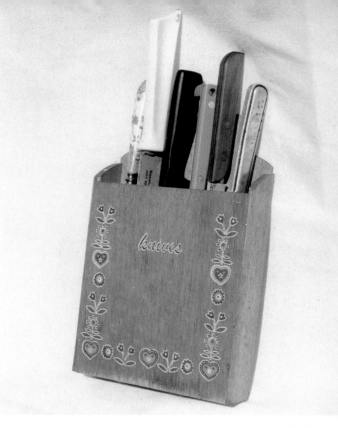

Late knife box. With knives $16-$19, without knives $5-$7

Older, cream-colored, pottery mixing bowl. $12-$15

Small sifter made to use over a measuring cup. $3-$5

Pie Bird used to let steam escape from pie. $25-$30

Two pie plates, one plain, the other with a fluted edge. $4-$6 each

Cast aluminum round roaster marked Wagner Ware. $15-$17

Cast aluminum oblong roaster made by Majestic Cookware. $17-19

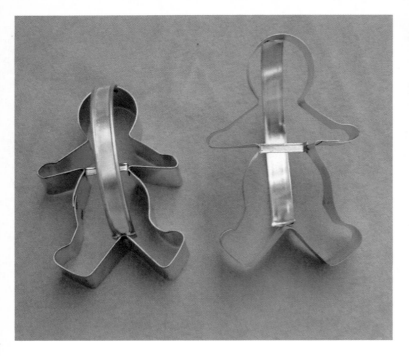

Two tin gingerbread men cookie cutters. $3-$4 each

Cast aluminum bundt pan. $15-$17

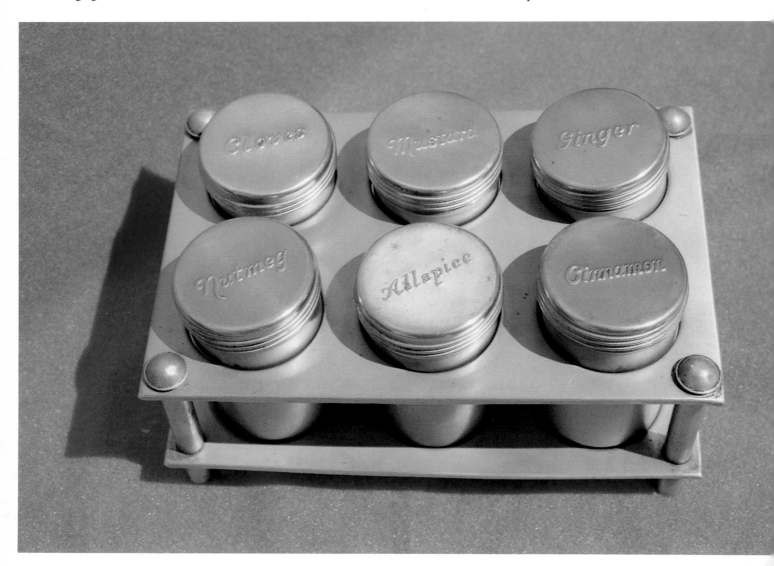

Spun aluminum spice rack offered for $1.35 in the 1909 Wear-Ever
catalogue. $18-$22

Electric hot water kettle. $17-$21

Large aluminum colander. $7-$9

Chapter Three
Baskets, Kitchen and Harvest

Once upon a time, not so long ago, the people, especially farm folk, had only three types of containers: handmade wooden buckets, barrels, and baskets. Of the three, only the baskets have remained in use, and their use has been severely hampered by the use of paper bags and cardboard boxes. But collectors still find baskets fascinating, although they don't seem to be as popular as they were a few years ago. One reason probably stems from the fact the fine old handmade baskets are getting harder and harder to find, and when found, their prices are quite high. Another is the fact so many new baskets are coming on the market, priced much more reasonably, and they seem to have a stronger appeal. After all, we don't use baskets exactly as our ancestors did, yet we still collect baskets of one kind or another — for nostalgia and to decorate our homes.

Baskets are known to have been used in every country in the world, and they were made of whatever materials were available in that country. Different countries have different types of trees, vines, and grasses, materials used in basketry. Each section of America has basketry materials, each different from the other. And in each area the people have different uses for their baskets. This accounts for the many types of baskets found today. The materials and the uses for which baskets were made, had much to do with their shapes. Then there were the makers, who made the final decisions as to the shapes.

People in nearly every country had chickens in those early days, so they needed baskets not only for gathering eggs but for taking them to the store to sell or barter for other foods. Since so many women made their own baskets, especially their egg baskets, it was not unusual for them to have two eggs bas-

kets — an old one for gathering and a fancy one to take to the nearby store. Even in those early days, the women had a tendency to try to outdo their neighbors. In this case by having the prettiest basket. In Eastern Tennessee and Kentucky, and maybe in other areas as well, it was not unusual for the women to carve intricate designs on the handles of their egg baskets. The type of egg basket depended somewhat on the area where it was made and used. For example, in the south the basket might be round or even square, but usually a rather plain basket, while in the middle of the country the buttocks basket was the most popular by far.

Eggs not only furnished one of the most needed foods, they also brought in a bit of cash when the extra eggs were sold. For that reason the housewife had to keep raising chickens, both for the eggs and for the meat. It was essential that she have good "setting hens," hens that would not only lay fertile eggs but ones that would "set" on the nest until the eggs were hatched. Another requirement for those good hens was that they take care of the baby chicks until they were able to take care of themselves. Not everybody had good setting hens, therefore the ones who did became quite popular in their neighborhoods because they was expected to loan their hens as soon as they had enough chicks to fill their needs. Often the hens were on the nest again, if they were especially good, which meant they had to be transported, both eggs and hen, to the neighbor with care. This created the need for another basket, a hen basket. Since the families might live miles apart, the hen in her basket often had to be transported on a horse, the only means of transportation the family might have. Those first hen baskets were designed to be carried near the neck of the horse, just in front of the saddle. The style of hen baskets never changed.

One of the reasons baskets became so popular in those early days — other than the fact they were the only containers available — was that they were used for both planting and harvesting. Whereas farmers once used baskets for carrying the seeds to the fields as well as for harvesting the crop, most of the farms are now mechanized. There are a few who continued to use their baskets as they always have, but their number has been decreasing rapidly since around 1960.

An egg basket is still essential for the people who raise a few chickens just for their own use. They prefer eggs from their own chickens to the "store boughten" ones. Then there are some women who continue to use their old clothes pin baskets when they hang the wash on the line. Usually this is not a specially-made basket, made just for the chore, but rather an old, worn one left over from other chores.

An unusual basket and one seldom seen now, unless a collection from an advanced collector goes on the market, is the waterproof basketry jug. In some areas as late as half a century ago, there wasn't an abundance of buckets or tin containers for carrying water from the springs and wells. This was especially true of the people of the arid sections of the southwest. The Apaches are credited with making the first woven water jugs as they were among the most skilled of the basketmakers, yet it is believed the Paiutes made the best waterproof jugs. They made jugs of willow and coated them with gum from the pinon trees to make them completely waterproof. The Havasupias are credited with making the first stand-up basketry jugs, the kind with the pointed bottoms so they would stand in the ground and not topple over, spilling the contents. The Cherokees also made a waterproof basketry jug, but they made theirs of double-woven river cane and coated it with bees wax.

Fruit drying basket, wide spaced splints. $75-$85

Half a century or so ago, bakeries were few and far between, especially in rural areas; therefore, the housewife had to bake the pies and cakes enjoyed by the family. And like all good cooks, she never missed a chance to show off her culinary skills. She would pack her finest cakes and pies in a pie basket and be off to a church gathering, a family reunion, or a picnic in the park. The pies might be meat or sweet and they might be packed in a single or double pie basket. The advantages of the double basket was the fact she could take two pies in one container. Today those baskets are seldom used for their original purpose, nor are they as avidly collected as they once were. Reasons for that could be scarcity and high prices. But there are still collectors who search for the pie baskets, even the later one, made by the Passamaquoddy Indians of the northeast.

Not only did the women have to bake pies and cakes, they also had to bake their own bread. It all started with the baking done in the iron Dutch ovens and the ovens built into the side of the old fireplaces. This custom continued for years, in fact it continued into the woodburning stove era. This baking of bread created the need for two types of baskets — the bread raising basket and the basketry bread tray. The Germans who settled in Pennsylvania are believed to have been the first to make the so-called dough or bread raising baskets. At that time they were usually known as Mennonite baskets and were generally made of rye in the coiled manner. As the custom spread to other areas, the basketmakers in those areas used whatever basketry materials were available. The dough had to have a

container in which to rise, so the baskets were used exclusively until the tin and later graniteware bread raisers were introduced. Some continued to use their baskets long after the others were introduced.

Wall baskets were and still are very useful, and they were probably made by every basketmaker who ever wove a splint or coiled a vine. Although everybody did not use them for the same purpose, nevertheless they were always considered one of the most useful baskets. Some were used for holding combs, others for brushes, while another group might use them to hold letters. In some homes they were used to hold the bobbins for the loom. Some families might have several wall baskets to be used for all the chores mentioned above along with some they had just devised.

There were also candle baskets, small, rather deep baskets that hung on the wall, usually in the kitchen, to hold the ever necessary candles. Remember, in the early days the only light in the house was either from the fireplace or from candles. Even when they obtained oil lamps, old habits were hard to break. And one just never knew when they might need a candle, so the candle baskets continued to hang on the wall. Today those old candle baskets are being painted bright colors to match the decor in modern kitchens. Collectors are also painting some of the newer baskets in bright colors and using them in their kitchens.

Until a few decades ago, no self respecting housewife would have felt worthy of the name unless she had at least one fruit-drying basket. The most popular of these, especially in apple growing areas, was naturally the apple drying basket. They were generally loosely woven flat baskets on which housewives spread sliced apples, or if they lived in peach country, housewives dried peaches. The sliced fruit, peeled or unpeeled, was placed on the basket, which allowed air to circulate through the open weave and dry the fruit. Depending on the weather a housewife might have dried fruit in a few weeks, fruit she could save for the long winters ahead.

Apparently basketmakers, like other specialized workers, became tired of making the same old baskets in the same old style, year after years, so they often made novelties. Like the early Indian basketmakers they made things with which they were familiar. In some case they made things used in the kitchen, including pitchers, either splint or reed.

For a century or so we have imported some excellent examples of basketry from the Philippines, and probably for the last half century we have gotten a variety of basketry items from China. The baskets from both countries are made of bamboo or reed so it is very easy to distinguish them from local baskets. On about half of them the workmanship is excellent, the price is very affordable, and the design attractive. Since the prices are so affordable, the collectors feel free to experiment with them by adding color and maybe new designs. In a few cases, the open weave trays may come with designs already embroidered on them while in others the collectors may add to them, or remove the designs and embroider completely new designs that matches their decor better. The same applies to the closely woven reed trays. Some come with a painted design while others are plain so the talented new owner can paint on her own design.

That perhaps is the fascination of all baskets. They allow the owner to choose her own colors and designs, and she can decided exactly how she wants to use and display her baskets.

That brings us to the ultimate choice — how to display one's collection. In old restored farm houses, baskets are most attractive when hung from the old wooden beams, or they can be displayed in old cabinets or hutches. When the collection outgrows the allotted space, the baskets can be beautifully displayed on old mitten dryers, the stand type with short dowel hangers, or on stands converted from late hat racks. The square post of the hat rack can have dowels added along the sides from top to bottom, and the baskets may be hung, double if necessary, on the dowels.

As proof that anything can be used to make baskets, this one is made of corn cobs. $8-$20 depending on the size of the basket

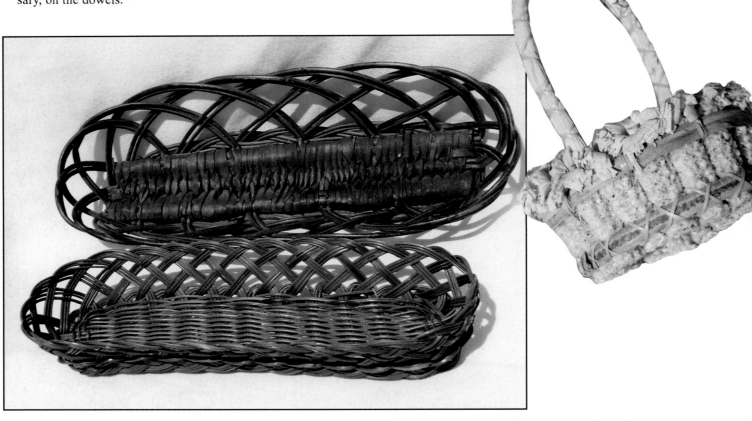

Women baked their own loaves of bread and made baskets in which to serve them. Woven baskets $9-$12 each

Embroidered bamboo basket, late. $10-$12

32

Hanging wall basket made by Penobscot Indian basketmaker. $40-$50

Picnic basket. Some came with early automobiles and will have the name of the car in the top. $25-$35

Splint basket with dyed splints at either end. Vine handle. $25-$30

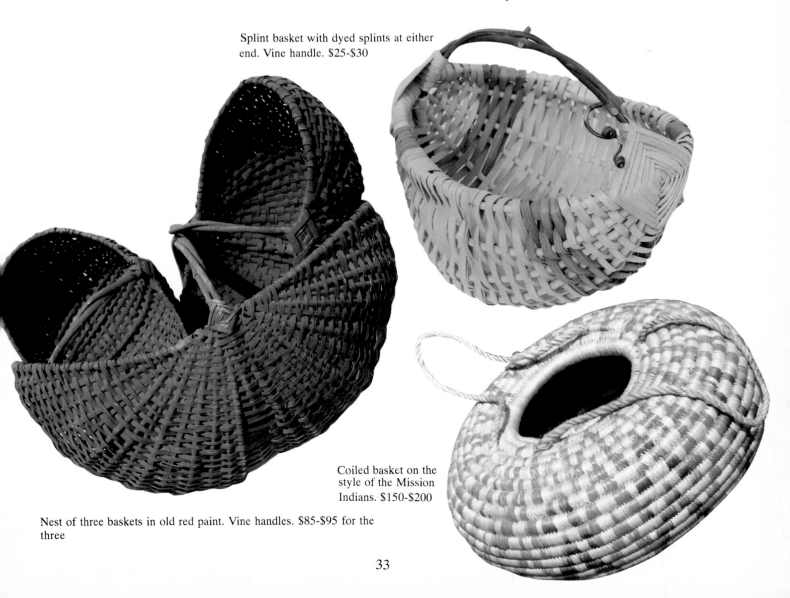

Coiled basket on the style of the Mission Indians. $150-$200

Nest of three baskets in old red paint. Vine handles. $85-$95 for the three

African-made, coiled basket in bright colors. $25-$35

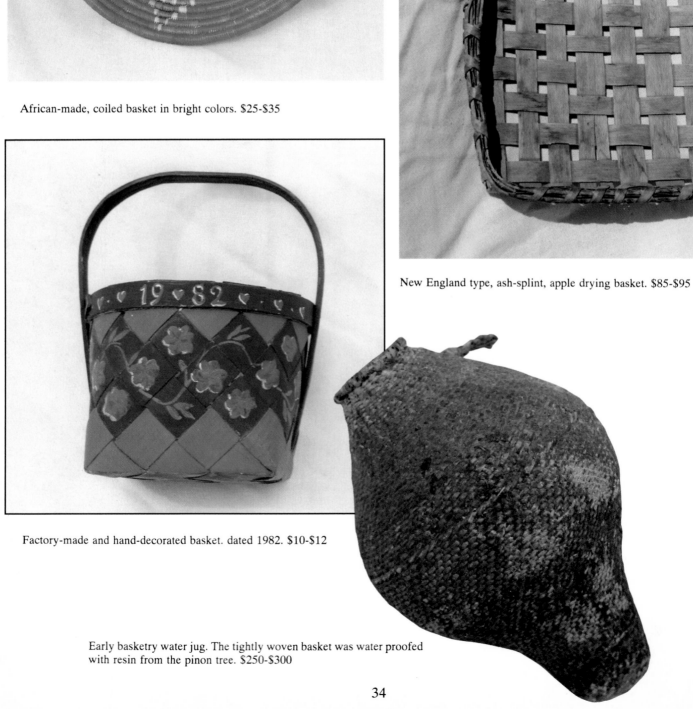

New England type, ash-splint, apple drying basket. $85-$95

Factory-made and hand-decorated basket. dated 1982. $10-$12

Early basketry water jug. The tightly woven basket was water proofed with resin from the pinon tree. $250-$300

34

Basketmakers often made novelties. Reed pitcher-shaped basketry item. $35-$40

Double pie basket with double swing handles made by the Passamaquoddy Indians. $125-$150

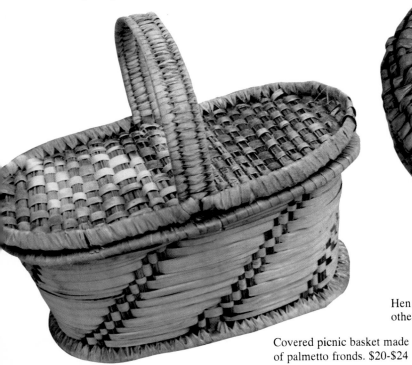

Hen basket used for transporting "setting" hens from one farm to another. $45-$60

Covered picnic basket made of palmetto fronds. $20-$24

Credited to the Shakers, but it is believed they only sold these baskets after buying them elsewhere. Due to the Shaker connection prices are very high. $150-$200

Seneca-made corn washing basket. $50-$75

Candle baskets hung on the wall making candles easy to find. This one is painted green to match the kitchen decor of a modern house. $18-$23

Two market baskets from the 1930s. One for the mother, the other for a child. $20-$25 for large, $15-$18 for small

Late, medium-sized, swing handle basket. $25-$30

Cherokee-made burden basket, white oak splints dyed with bloodroot and walnut. Chief's Daughter design. $200-$350

Called a dish drainer basket by the original family, the one who made it. People made baskets to fit their own needs a few years ago. Made of vines. $35-$50

Small swing handle basket painted green to match kitchen decor. $20-$26

Cherokee-made storage basket, made of river cane, dyed with walnut and bloodroot. Approximately 12 inches in diameter at the widest point, 13 inches tall. $200-$400

Back pack made in the Philippines of finely cut strips of bamboo. Brought back by visitors because they were so light and easy to use. Circa 1930. $85-$95

Storage basket made from materials found along the Nile River in Africa. $65-$85

Navajo peach basket. $200-$300

Late bamboo basket with God's Eye (folded square to reinforce the handles where they fasten into the basket), vine handle. $20-$25

Market basket painted pale blue and touched with gold for modern decorator look. $23-$27

Large ash splint storage basket. Could have been made by either the Penobscot or Passamaquoddy Indians of Maine. $200-$250.

Deeper, woven winnowing basket. $27-$32

Shallow winnowing basket, woven. $25-$30

Old mitten dryers are ideal for displaying smaller baskets.

Chapter Four
Butter and Cheese Tools

Without the same dependence on cattle that our ancestors had, it is difficult for us to even imagine the many ways cattle helped to feed families in the past or to supply some of their needs. There are a large number of tools and utensils associated with those cattle of yesteryear that are still available to collectors. Chances are no other animal has left us so many things to collect, some of which we may not even want to collect. But first we have to remember how many things were derived from the cow. In the first place she had a new calf every year. Now it would either become another milk cow, or, if a male, would become either meat for the table or an ox to pull the wagon or plow. We can't associate the oxens' yokes, pokes, and muzzles with kitchen antiques, nevertheless they are part of the cattle collectibles. Later the branding iron became a part of those collectibles, but it really isn't remotely related to kitchen antiques and collectibles.

Actually it wasn't the cow or the milk that left us so many desirable antiques and collectibles, but rather the by-products like butter and cheese. Of course there are the many interesting things connected with the milk like the three-legged milking stools, milk buckets, milk cans including the very popular graniteware examples, the funnels, and the strainers. Later there would be the glass milk bottles that are sought after by some collectors, but none of these compare with the popularity or the abundance of butter molds.

It would be an almost impossible task today to find one person, collector or non-collector, who doesn't have at least one butter mold. When they only have one mold, it has generally been handed down from family to family. Then there are some collectors who have dozens of molds while some have hundreds. The latter are not as plentiful as those with a dozen or so. Butter mold collectors have to be more careful now than they were a decade or so ago as new butter molds have been and still are being made in Canada and brought into the United States. It is possible they are also being made in other countries and brought in, but we are not familiar with them. Canadian examples are plentiful in the northeast. It is relatively easy to spot the new ones as the design is so weakly done. Reports are they are being aged in various ways from being buried in manure to being darkened with strong tea, but the design itself tells the tale. Designs on the new molds seen so far do not even resemble the older ones as the carving or design is so shallow.

Before the butter could be made, the sour milk had to be churned and that chore alone has left us a variety of antiques and collectibles that rivals the number of butter molds. At first the churns were made of wood, usually cedar with wooden bands. Later they used brass bands as well as different kinds of wood.

Reports are that in some countries the milk was churned by putting it in some kind of skin, hanging the skin on a flexible limb, and swinging it back and forth until the butter came to the top. But in America churns seem to be the choice for making butter. First, there were the wooden ones, then the stoneware, the swinging wooden ones, the brass, and finally the glass Dazey churns. One reason churns are not quite as popular as other cattle-related antiques is that the wooden ones have to be filled with water from time to time to keep the wood swollen and in place, otherwise they will shrink and fall apart as most wooden things of that shape have a tendency to do. Another reason they are only semi-popular is the size. Some are pretty large, and it is hard to display them when space is limited.

Once the butter was made, the tedious chore of washing it (that is, getting the remaining milk out) began. This chore left us quite a few collectibles including butter paddles, ladles, and the wooden or pottery bowls used to get the butter ready to mold, or in some cases ready to ship.

In the very early days the farm wife packed her excess butter in buckets and tubs and shipped it by train to the city, often to a grocer who had agreed to buy it. If she sold it to the local store, the sales could be small as the majority of people in the area had at least one cow which meant they would only be buying milk and butter for the couple of months their cow was dry, the short time before her new calf was born. Or she might sell to her neighbor, eliminating the grocer. If the family lived close to the nearest town, there was a possibility the housewife would mold all her butter and take it into town once a week where she delivered it to regular customers. Although these sales do not sound exciting, nevertheless they left us two types of antiques, neither of which is plentiful today. But that should not cause any worry as they are not the most sought after. One is the bucket or tub in which butter was packed for shipping on the train. Usually it only had the name of the contents, butter, and the name of the shipper and the receiver. Another is the paper wrappers used to wrap the molded butter. These wrappers, usually about 7 by 10 inches for the half pound size, were printed alike and sold to the farm wife who only milked a few cows. On one particular type it simply specified the product, the weight, and left a blank space for the seller to add her name. In those days some had to tendency to describe a 4 or 5 cow herd as a dairy.

Briefly describing butter molds in a chapter on kitchen antiques and collectibles when it would be difficult to cover them completely in a book is sort of like glossing over the subject. Just saying they are round, square, and oblong in size isn't

Plunger from half pound, round butter mold. Rose hip design. $60-$75 for complete mold

that were the cheap ones or the giveaways. No matter what kind they were, they included a butter dish because butter was an important part of every meal. Margarine had not yet been introduced and even when it was offered to the public about 40 years ago the majority of people continued to use butter which made the butter dish essential on every table.

But it was in glass that thousands, maybe millions, of butter dishes were made. In the hey-day of pressed or pattern glass, about 1875 to 1915 (later for some patterns), there was hardly a pattern made that did not include a butter dish. Some were inordinately fancy while others were very plain, but they were all sold and used. With so many people, families were large in those days, eating three meals a day at home, it was the custom to keep the essentials, butter, sugar, cream, and spoons, in holders, usually in a matching pattern, on the table. The table might be "set" with flatware, but there were always extras on the table in case they were needed. These four-piece sets consisting of a butter dish, sugar dish, creamer, and spooner were advertised and sold as sets. Butter was so widely used and the butter dish so popular, some very unusual single ones were made although they are a bit difficult to find today, and quite expensive. Later long, narrow butter dishes would be made to hold the quarter pound sticks of margarine or creamery butter. Butter pats were also popular. They were made to hold either the butter molded in the miniature molds or a slice off the quarter pound stick. Incidently, butter pats can be found in china, pattern, or cut glass.

Butter was not the only by-product of milk; there was also cheese. In the early years when so many families lived on the farm, nearly everybody made cheese. The few who didn't, usually bought it from a neighbor who made extra cheese to sell along with the excess butter. It was another way for the housewife to make a little money.

The making of cheese left quite a few antiques and collectibles worth owning. Some are rather plentiful now while others are next to non-existent. Then there are some pieces like the large cheese presses that have little collecting value except to those restoring old farmsteads or museums. There are also a few people who still make their own cheese and the presses are valuable to them to be used again as they were previously. With the back to the land movement several years ago, the presses were salvaged by people who wanted to make cheese just as their ancestors did.

Among the cheese making antiques and collectibles are the curd breakers, often handmade, that were used to break up the curds after the milk had clabbered making it easier to use. After the milk had soured, it turned into a solid mass that was described as "clabbered." Another sought after, scarce, and expensive cheese related antique is the so-called cheese basket. It was woven with hexagon shaped holes because the cheese makers found this style more suited to their work. The same pottery or wooden bowls used in butter making could be used in cheese making. In the small tool category there were the cheese testers, cheese scoops, and slicers.

enough because they vary so much more. The round ones can be divided into still other categories like the pound, half pound, and miniature sizes used to make individual servings, especially for dinner parties. Regardless of shape, most of the molds were made in both pound and half pound sizes. The square molds could be the so-called hotel or commercial styles, or they might be the fancy pound and half pound sizes used by the families or the small dairies. The hotel and commercial names were the ones given the factory-made molds when they were advertised in old catalogs. Generally the half pound size is easier to find, indicating it was more widely used in those days. It also seems to be the most popular size, probably because more of that size are available. For the dedicated collector, the design seems more important than the size. Old hand carved designs of cows, eagles, pineapples, and swans are the most desirable and the most sought after. But there isn't a butter mold collector alive who can pass up a mold with any good design including those with flowers, wheat, and initials.

Glass butter molds were shown in some of the old catalogs, those from around the turn of the century, but they were still being made again about 20 to 25 years ago. They are still being made. The designs on both the old and the new, at least those we have seen, are a fleur-de-lis on one and a cow on the other. The old ones and the early reproductions were all made in clear glass, but not long ago one was seen in a good shade of medium blue glass with a cow design, exactly like the earlier ones except for the color of the glass.

If the housewife went to the trouble of molding butter, and most of them did even for family use, then she was definitely going to keep it in a pretty butter dish. Like everything else in those days, butter dishes came in a variety of materials including aluminum, silver, silver plate, china, and glass. Nearly every pattern of china included a butter dish in the set. This was not only the fine old Haviland, but also the sets of dishes

Four section butter mold. $110-$125

Handmade, wooden cow bell. Rather than a central clapper inside, this one has two clappers, one on either side. $95-$115

Half pound, round butter mold with pineapple design. $65-$75

Large wooden butter paddle. $39-$45

Pair of wooden butter workers or paddles. $29-$35

43

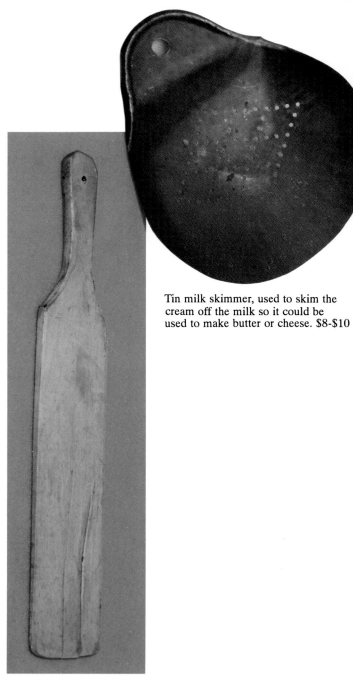

Tin milk skimmer, used to skim the cream off the milk so it could be used to make butter or cheese. $8-$10

Silk with a picture of a cow. Often found in dairy products during the early part of this century. $20-$25

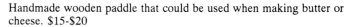

Handmade wooden paddle that could be used when making butter or cheese. $15-$20

Dairy size tin strainer used to strain the milk into five and ten gallon cans during the 1930s and '40s. $10-$12

½ POUND   CHOICE   NET WEIGHT

DAIRY   BUTTER

Put up by_____

These waxed paper wrappers could be bought by people who wanted to wrap their butter to sell. $1-$2 each

Silver plated, Victorian butter dish. $25-$30

Same butter dish open.

Large butter worker. Probably used by a small dairy. $150-$200

Patterned or pressed glass butter dish, holds round molded, half pound of butter. $45-$60

Individual butter molds, make designed butter pats that fit small butter pats. $25-$35 depending on age

Early milk glass milk pitcher, painted design on side. Circa 1890. $115-$135

Late aluminum butter dish for sticks of butter or oleo. Buelinum trademark. $16-$22

Wooden based cheese slicer in original box. $15-$18

Late milk pitcher in the shape of what appears to be a rooster. $15-$18

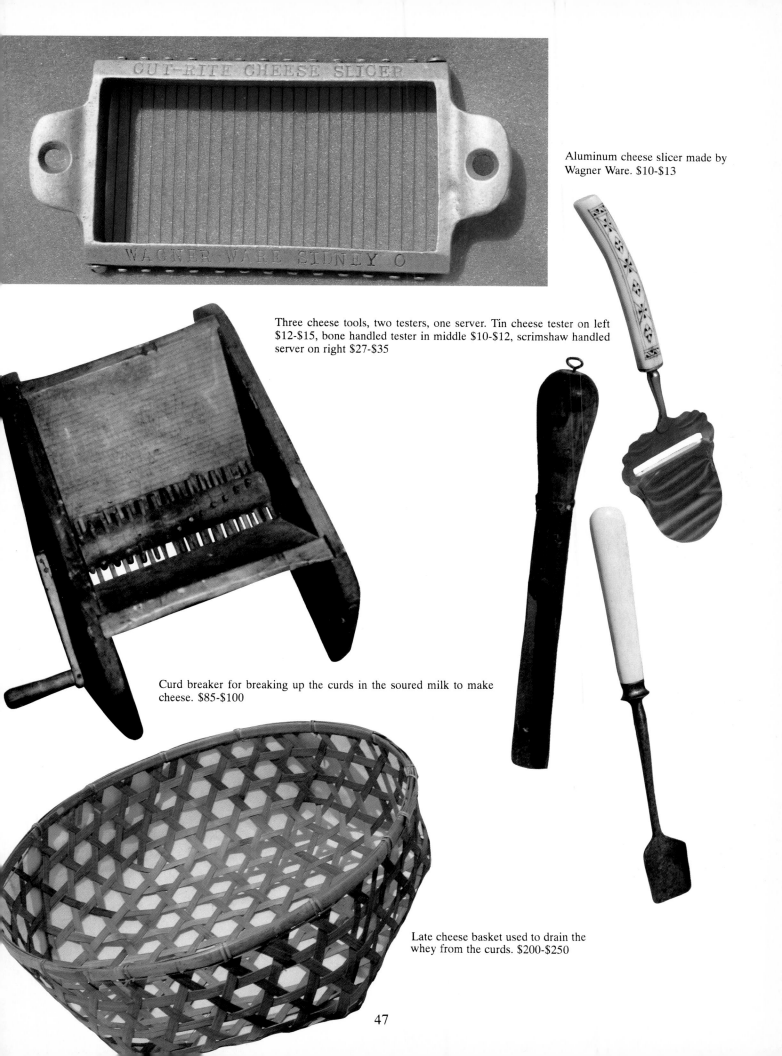

Aluminum cheese slicer made by Wagner Ware. $10-$13

Three cheese tools, two testers, one server. Tin cheese tester on left $12-$15, bone handled tester in middle $10-$12, scrimshaw handled server on right $27-$35

Curd breaker for breaking up the curds in the soured milk to make cheese. $85-$100

Late cheese basket used to drain the whey from the curds. $200-$250

47

Chapter Five
Chafing Dishes

While searching for the invention or the ancestry of chafing dishes, it was found that some seem to think this dish evolved from the brazier that was used in ancient Babylonian and Egyptian homes. Actually the ancient brazier was a metal pan on legs that was used as a portable heater to warm various rooms of the house. Its use has been recorded in old carvings and paintings as well as in a few tapestries. Then there are records of its use in the Orient, in fact there are some who believe it originated there.

As time passed, so did the function of the brazier. It was no longer used exclusively to warm a room; it was now used to cook food. That meant the same charcoal would heat the room and cook a meal. As its usefulness grew, so did its popularity. By the 16th century, the brazier was being used in many countries in Europe. The English soon found how useful it could be. There is a chance that by that time — around the 17th century — it was being used more for cookery than for heating, but it was still likely to have been used for both chores.

By the 18th century, the brazier had left the floor and been installed on the table to make the cooking easier, no doubt. That change also created a name change. The new name was table stove. Shortly thereafter it became known as a chafing dish. The name change gave it so much prestige that both English and American silversmiths began making handsome examples. With such fine examples available, it was understandable how the acceptance of the chafing dish spread. Chafing dishes were as warmly welcomed into the homes of British aristocracy as they were in the finer Colonial homes of America.

Through those years first one and then another inventive mind had a go at improving the old brazier, but it only took one man, Alexis Soyer, to make the chafing dish really famous. He was a gifted young French chef who went to London during the mid-19th century to manage a club belonging to a famous gourmet society. It was said that his winning personality, great charm, and sincerity along with his superb meals attracted all the social greats from the artistic world. He wasn't too happy with the so-called table stove of that time so he set about creating one that would best fit his needs. He added a second pan for hot water and an alcohol lamp for heat. He wanted to make it possible to prepare certain dishes at the table — in the presence of the guests. His idea, it seems, was to impress them, and apparently it worked as the Soyer chafing dish became an instant success.

Another group believes the chafing dish actually began with the Soyer invention and the brazier had little or nothing to do with it. Regardless of its origin, the chafing dish was here to stay. It became an integral part of gracious entertaining, and it also won a place in the finer restaurants. But its popularity in home entertaining waned during the early part of the 20th century. The automobile was partly to blame as the auto made it possible for the affluent young men to take their dates out to theatres and restaurants, provided, of course, they lived in a city large enough to provide those things. In rural areas, small towns, and villages, the young ladies still entertained their young men with intimate suppers and fancy desserts, often prepared in the chafing dish. This gave the girls an excellent opportunity to show off their culinary skills, and in those days a young man was duly impressed with a young lady who could cook and was a gracious hostess. She would make a good wife.

About this time Manning, Bowman & Company, Meriden, Connecticut published an undated booklet of "Recipes for the Chafing Dish." One of the most interesting things in this booklet, other than the recipes, is a small, half page note added to the last page. It is an announcement of the Ivory Enameled Food Pan that was patented May 23, 1899, and used in the top of their chafing dishes. They described it as the best article ever made for the chafing dish. These chafing dishes are now of special interest to several groups. One group is the graniteware collectors while the other is the group that wants to use their old chafing dish and feel that the graniteware pan is safer for food than the other types.

The first page of the Manning, Bowman & Company booklet gives instructions on using a chafing dish. This is especially helpful for collectors who are now buying the older chafing dishes in antique malls, flea market, and auctions as these usually come without instructions. They suggested that the lamp be filled and lighted. Put at least a half pint of water in the water pan, they said, more for some dishes. Mixtures requiring slow cooking or those that burned easily, should always be cooked over hot water, they explained. If more heat was needed as in broiling, the water pan should be removed and the food pan placed directly over the fire or lamp. Later electric chafing dishes would be made which made regulating the heat a much easier chore. One of the most important things, they stressed, was the fact the hostess who planned to serve a variety of dishes cooked in chafing dishes would need several as two or three might not be enough. That helps explain why there are so many available today. They also listed the pieces necessary for a complete chafing dish outfit. Of course the first thing was the chafing dish itself, then a tray on which to place it, a spoon, fork, and skimmer, all made especially for use with the dish. A toaster, cutlet dish, and flagon for the alcohol completed the outfit.

Flagon for filling the stoves or burners under the chafing dishes. $15-$20

It was not necessary for the dish to be heated with alcohol lamps as canned heat made a good substitute. The pan might be made of copper lined with tin, aluminum, chrome, or stainless steel. Other than copper the stand and the pans could be made of brass, aluminum, chrome, silver, and silver plate. The handles could be of any material including stag horns. On the very large, expensive dishes there might be two to four lamps. There were also numerous accessories including soup units, crepe pans, toasters, and cutlet dishes that could be added to the original unit so other dishes could be prepared easily.

And there were recipes for preparing dishes that now almost boggle the mind. One of those dishes was Salmi of Woodcock. The list of ingredients included two woodcocks, bits of fat pork, two minced button onions, two pinches (remember this was a circa 1900 recipe) of salt, juice of two lemons, two gills of wine, and buttered toast. Another recipe was for Frog Saddles. For this recipe the cook needed frog's legs, three tablespoons butter, one gill of cream, pepper, salt, and nutmeg. The butter was melted in the chafing dish, a little flour added, and it was stirred until the mixture was smooth. The cream was added and then the frog's legs that had been seasoned with pepper, salt, and nutmeg. The dish was covered and cooked for 20 minutes. A recipe for an egg dish required one gill of rich gravy, five eggs, one tablespoon of butter, one tablespoon minced parsley, half teaspoon salt, and half salt spoon white pepper. According to the recipe the melted butter and gravy were mixed in the chafing dish and when the mixture was "hissing hot" the beaten eggs were stirred in and cooked until they thickened.

Information on how to cook the various dishes was given. For example, information was given in each recipe on whether the food should be cooked using both pans, or if only the blazer or pan was necessary. Both pans were necessary, they said, to prepare a dish called Terrapin a la Pennsylvania. Ingredients for this one consisted of two 8-inch, cow terrapins, yolk of four hard boiled eggs, fourth pound of butter, half pint of cream, and half a gill of good sherry.

Judging by the recipes it would appear any dish from the simple to the most intricate could be prepared in the chafing dish. And the way they described it, it sounds so easy. There were recipes for smelts, lobster patties, and curried lobster, as well as Lobster a la Newberg. The recipe for Chicken Halibut was probably one of the most interesting as chicken was not used at all except in the title. Ingredients consisted of a cupful of cold, boiled halibut, two hard boiled eggs, cup and a half of milk, butter the size of an egg, crumbs of four crackers, catsup, salt and pepper. (We have to remember that cooking terms like the size of a walnut or the size of an egg were used to describe some ingredients before Fannie Farmer standardized amounts.) The halibut was shredded with a fork and set aside. The milk was put into the food pan with water in the water pan, and the milk brought to a boil. While it was boiling the butter, catsup, salt, pepper, and cracker crumbs were added. Then the halibut was added. It was allowed to cook for five minutes before the finely chopped eggs were added. It was then served on a hot platter with bits of buttered toast. Other recipes in the booklet included Grilled Sweet Potatoes, Creamed Potatoes, Lamb or Mutton Curry, Fricassee of Dried Beef, Roast Beef Chauffé, Broiled Sweetbreads, Welsh Rarebit, and Pinou-chi which was a candy. There were also recipes for invalids like Beef Broth and Flour Gruel.

Chafing dishes were so popular and some so ornate that one of the latter, an unsigned, whimsical Arts and Crafts copper example with rabbits holding the pans sold at auction for $1,200 in 1993. In 1994 an Arts and Crafts chafing table or stand, one made especially for the chafing dish, sold for several thousand dollars.

It would be difficult to class the Korean Bul-Ko-Ki as a chafing dish, nor is it exactly like the old braziers; however, the Bul-Ko-Ki is used to cook food at the table which puts it on the fringe of the chafing dish category — later than some, perhaps, but still in the same general category. It is a very interesting piece, and this one has a list of instructions — how to use it and how to prepare the meat that will be cooked. The instructions do suggest using charcoal for the cooking, but said any kind of heat could be used including gas. The recipe for seasoning what they called "raw beef" is 10 teaspoons sugar, 4 ounces soy sauce, 3 cloves garlic, teaspoon pepper, 2 teaspoons bean oil, salt, and prepared sesame seeds. Three pounds of beef, enough to feed five people, was kept in this mixture for 30 to 40 minutes, the longer the better, before putting it on top of the Bul-Ko-Ki to barbecue.

Another cooking-serving dish that is not really a chafing dish, but one that fits nicely on the fringe of the category is the buffet serving dish. It is much later than the chafing dishes described in the booklet of recipes. In fact, the buffet serving dish seemed to reach the peak of its popularity around the Forties and Fifties. It is still quite popular at large affairs where the foods must be kept warm. Usually found in either silver plate or maybe nickel, they are very attractive. Instead of the metal cooking pans, these have Pyrex or Fire King pans.

Chafing dish with graniteware food pan. Very sought after today. $45-$50

Chafing dish open showing the graniteware food pan.

Chafing dish with slightly different legs. $28-$32

Many chafing dishes are quite similar; only the legs, handles, finials, and the burner will be different. The quality of the material used to make them plus the workmanship may be extremely different, hence the variations in price. $28-$33

Nickel plated chafing dish on tray. $38-$47

Chafing dish with tray. $35-$45

Copper chafing dish with black legs and aluminum band. $24-$30

Large brass chafing dish, 15 inches in diameter. Very plain. $29-$33

Regular size copper and brass chafing dish with a miniature duplicate that is believed to be a salesman's sample. Regular size $25-$28, miniature $65-$75

Ornate silver plated chafing dish. $35-$45

Plain chafing dish with bowed legs. $22-$28

Brass Korean Bul-Ko-Ki, not a chafing dish, but very similar and very collectible. $20-$25

Chafing dish was originally nickel plated over brass. Now worn down to the brass in spots. $18-$23

Ornate brass chafing dish and tray with pewter finial and ornaments on the cover. $50-$65

Brass chafing dish and tray. $38-$45

Copper and brass chafing dish. $20-$24

Copper and brass chafing dish, slightly different from the one above. $20-$24

Fancy hammered aluminum chafing dish. Unmarked, but probably made by Everlast. $38-$55

Silver plate chafing dish with ornate rim and legs. $38-$45

Aluminum chafing dish, Buenilum trademark. $30-$35

Aluminum chafing dish, Rodney Kent Silver Company trademark. $30-$35

Buffet Server. Not exactly a chafing dish, but a later version that served practically the same purpose. Was much fancier. $50-$60

Buffet server with two food containers. $45-$65

Late, metal, Sears buffet server. $5-$8

56

Chapter Six
Coffee Making

Our society has changed so much in the past several decades, it is sometimes difficult to remember exactly how things were done in that other era. One thing that has stayed consistent is the drinking of coffee. Today most home have a coffee maker, and they likely also use instant coffee. Several decades ago it was an entirely different story. Then the housewife might have as many as half a dozen coffee pots. Some were for the actual making while others were used only for serving.

Coffee is said to have been discovered by an Ethiopian goat herder named Kaldi around 850 A.D. But there were no special pots for brewing it for a long time. According to legend everybody simply brewed the grounds in water until it smelled good. That didn't take long. The maker then strained the grounds out of the coffee using whatever method she had devised. Around 1800 a French pharmacist named R. Descroisilles invented the biggin. It was a utensil that consisted of two slender metal containers separated by a plate filled with holes that served as a filter. At that time it was made either of tin, copper, or pewter. It would be about 50 years before it became available in graniteware. Then it would be nearly another 25 years before anyone in America applied for a biggin patent.

Around the turn of the twentieth century and earlier, most of the coffee pots being used in America were simply pots for boiling the ground coffee in water to make a delicious-smelling, great-tasting beverage. During that time coffee was purchased, in most cases, in green bean form, and roasted in the oven of the old woodburning stove. Each morning enough roasted coffee beans were ground in the old coffee mill to make coffee for the day. They didn't have a choice of fine or coarse grind as there was no setting on those old coffee mills. They ground it all the same.

The next step was the invention of the percolator, a pot that was still used on the stove, but in this case the water bubbled up and dripped through the coffee grounds rather than boiling it all together. Shortly after the introduction of the percolator, electricity became available in most cities and large towns. Since a few towns, villages, and all the rural areas did not get electricity until much later, the popularity of the electric percolator grew slowly in those areas. The next step, it is believed, was the introduction of the drip coffee maker that works exactly as the name implies — boiling water drips over the coffee as it finds its way from the bottom compartment to the top and back again.

The exact date the coffee pot originated is hard to track down, but it seems to have stemmed not so much from the love of the brewed beverage as from defiance, a desire to flout the rules. Of course this rebellion against authority has a long history, in fact, it began with Eve. A prime example of this disobedience began in England around 1647 when Parliament decreed it was illegal to drink coffee. At that time there was a group so totally convinced coffee was not only harmful to the person drinking it but to society at large, believing that coffee would definitely cause the drinkers to "dwindle into a succession of apes and pygmies," that they pressured Parliament into passing the law. Then there was another group, women who thought their husbands were spending entirely too much time at the coffee houses, who joined forces with those who thought coffee was harmful to one's health. Together these two groups were able to convince those in power that it would be to their advantage to declare coffee drinking illegal. As would be expected, that declaration was short lived.

What the people in power failed to recognize was the fact that when anything is declared illegal it becomes more popular than ever. Coffee drinking was no exception. The conditions then were somewhat like those created in this country when Prohibition was enacted. In both cases people who had never given a thought to alcohol or coffee just had to try it. Statistics on alcoholic beverage consumption during Prohibition are not available, but reports are coffee drinking increased several hundred times what it was before it was outlawed. Seems people just wanted to flout the ban, and flout it they did. They began drinking coffee at home as well as in the now shadowy coffee houses. Since it was banned, coffee couldn't be served openly so it was served in some of the most unlikely containers, somewhat like the booze that was served in coffee cups during prohibition. Whether the ban on coffee drinking was lifted, or simply ignore until it was forgotten is unknown, but it is known that the growing popularity of coffee increased the demand for coffee pots and drinking vessels.

Dutch sailors are credited with carrying coffee plants, originally a native of Africa, to Arabia. From there coffee moved on to Java, India, and Brazil, and finally around the world, probably being moved each time by sailors.

It is unlikely the average collector will ever see, much less find, one of the very early coffee pots. And few would want to except for research purposes. They are described as being "shaped like a tapering cylinder with a lid in the form of a cone, rather like the manner of the old type lanterns." Any pots over a century old are rather scarce, but there is an abundance of the later ones, especially the electric examples made from around 1930. The variety of materials used to make them is mind boggling. They can be found made of silver, china, silver plate, brass, copper, tin, pewter, pottery, graniteware, aluminum, and glass. Or they may have been made in a combinations of materials like one shown in the illustrations. Five different materials were used in making this pot, copper, brass, pewter for the spout, ebony for the handle, and a glass knob on top. The styles and materials will vary from pot to pot, but the shapes remain pretty much the same. Of course the most desirable coffee pots are the silver ones. They are not as plentiful as those made of other materials and the silver ones, especially the sterling silver ones, can be quite expensive. The coffee pots with a silver appearance found today will most likely be silver plate, or maybe nickel over copper. The nickel on so many of these has been stripped that there is a greater chance of finding copper pots, the ornate type, than nickel.

For collectors of genuine antiques, those 100 years old and older, these pots, especially the electric examples, will seem late. But we have to remember, few companies were producing silver products before around 1845. Prior to that time most silver items were being produced by independent silversmiths like Paul Revere and Hester Bateman. Many of those silversmiths continued to ply their trade after the manufacturers began making silver and silver plated items.

It may be difficult sometimes for the novice to distinguish between the pots that were made for the different beverages, like coffee, tea, and hot chocolate. Some were made with straight sides, others with a tapering cylinder shape, but one of the most popular styles seems to have been the pyriform or pear shape. Perhaps the easiest way to learn the difference is by study and comparison. Just remember nothing is carved in stone, and if you should make a mistake and use the wrong pot for a beverage, it is not a hanging crime.

The rich southern planters and merchants could afford to buy the exquisite cut glass coffee pots for use in their homes, in fact they were necessary for the gracious living they enjoyed. The settlers moving westward took another approach to their coffee making. They bought and used graniteware coffee pots, generally the large kind where the coffee grounds were boiled in the water and strained before drinking. The grounds could be left in the pot and with more water a new batch of coffee could be made at night. They used the pots on the trail and when the cabin was built, the pots were used near the fireplace or on the woodburning stove. The advantage of the graniteware pot was in the fact that it would not break, chip maybe, but not break. Nor would graniteware pots tarnish which meant there was little need for polishing, just enough to get the soot off that adhered from the open fire. But perhaps the thing they liked most about these pots was the cost. They were very inexpensive.

Cowboys found the graniteware coffee pot perfect for their lifestyle. It could be rinsed after coffee was made in the morning, and packed in the saddlebags until it was needed for the next meal. These pots not only helped to win the west, they moved right into the middle class dining rooms when they began to be made in fancy shapes with pewter handles and lids. Some even came with matching oil burning heaters so the coffee would stay hot for a long time — or it could be reheated easily.

The majority of avid collectors today are young and as collectors have always done, they are searching for things they remember from their childhood, mostly things they remember seeing at grandmother's house. Their grandmothers have more than likely discarded their old graniteware, and maybe their silver as well as their cut glass coffee pots in favor of the newer electric pots that came along during the last half century. The first electric percolators were introduced in 1908 by Landers, Frary, and Clark. Within a quarter century the country was saturated with electric coffee pots of all kinds. Their trademark was Universal, and others who joined them were Knapp-Monarch, Dover, S. W. Farber, General Electric, Porcelier who made some of the porcelain coffee pots, and the Continental Silver Company that made some of the fine examples of electric, aluminum percolators. Then there was Silex, along with others, who made the glass drip coffee makers with the little electric stoves or hot plates to be used with them.

There are also some plain coffee pots waiting to be collected along with espresso coffee makers, usually from Italy and Spain. Don't forget the many different cups and saucers that are definitely coffee related. No collection of coffee pots would be complete without some cups and saucers. In fact, every set of dishes, from Haviland to the most inexpensive, always includes a cup and saucer with each place setting. Even the inexpensive china given as premiums at gas stations and some stores in the Forties and Fifties included cups and saucers. Then there is the china from Southern Potteries of Irwin, Tennessee that is so collectible now. It was made by the carloads and shipped all over the country. In the Fifties people would stop along the highway at displays of what looked like mountains of china. Southern Potteries sold their china for 5 and 10 cents per piece. If you were lucky you got a cup and saucer for 5 cents, sometimes you had to pay 10 cents for the set. These china sales along the highways could have been the beginning of flea markets.

Espresso coffee pots from Italy and Spain. Small $5-$8, large $6-$9

Electric, hammered aluminum coffee pot. $15-$19

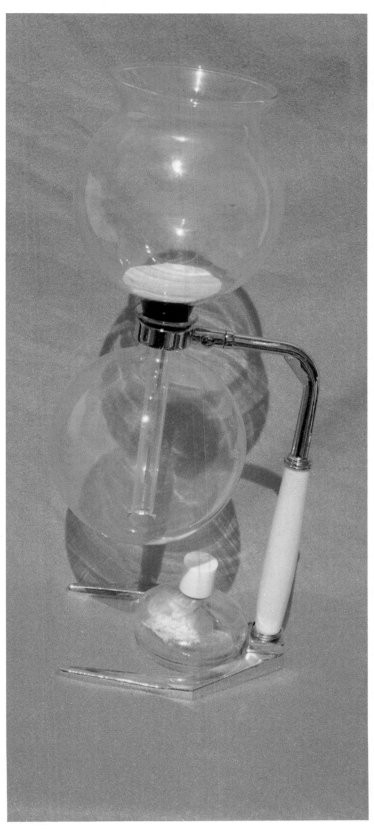

Pyrex coffee maker, Hellem Prestige make, has burner-like chafing dishes underneath. Instructions in French. $35-$45

Hand painted china cup and saucer, both pieces signed by the artist. $12-$15

Royal Rochester, electric coffee maker in five materials, brass base, copper body, pewter spout, ebony handle, and glass top. Made by Robeson Rochester Company, Rochester, New York. $40-$50

Coffee pot with spun aluminum top and aluminum decoration on the glass bottom. Small electric heater. $18-$23

When top is removed the bottom makes a perfect server.

Two Universal electric coffee pots of the 1930s and '40s. Small $8-$9, large $9-$12

Fancy coffee maker for serving at big, family meals or at parties. $25-$30

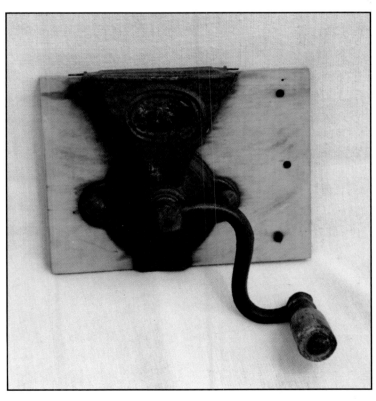

Iron coffee mill or grinder was very popular in the 1920s. $27-$35.

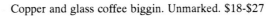

Copper and glass coffee biggin. Unmarked. $18-$27

Porcelier Manufacturing Company's porcelain, electric coffee percolator, $40-$50

Universal, trade name of Landers, Frary, and Clark, thermos pitcher for serving hot or cold beverages indoors or out. Patent dates from 1910 to 1916. $19-$24

When the cock crowed it was time to make coffee using this electric
Silex coffee maker. $22-$28

All aluminum electric drip-o-lator. $8-$10

Universal (Landers, Frary, and Clark) percolator with patent dates from
1912 to 1924. $10-$12

Old tin coffee pot, the type used on kerosene or wood burning stoves. $22-$28

These late Corning Ware percolators are becoming collectible. $12-$18 for either size

Unusual Corning Ware percolator with element inside. $12-$15

Coffee service, tray, creamer, sugar, and urn with white handles. $75-$85

Heavy cast aluminum drip-o-lator, Super-Maid Cookware trademark. $15-$20

Coffee service, coffee urn, tray, creamer, and sugar. $55-$75

Universal (Landers, Frary, and Clark) nickel plated thermos bottle. Patent dates 1914-1916. $18-$24

Pyrex coffee pot. $8-$10

Small, electric, aluminum coffee maker. $13-$18

Electric coffee urn with sugar and creamer. $40-$50

Glass coffee maker on small electric stove or heater. $12-$17

Large Staffordshire cup made by Adams, England. $95-$115

Opposite side of Staffordshire cup.

Electric coffee maker from the Art Deco period. $15-$18

French, aluminum coffee biggin, stacks together when not in use. $10-$12

Aluminum top, porcelain bottom drip-o-later made by The Enterprise Aluminum Company, Massillon, Ohio. $35-$40

Although it fits and makes coffee, this appears to be made of the parts of two coffee makers. The top is one type of glass with a design while the bottom is lighter weight and plain. $10-$12

Chapter Seven
Copper, Brass, Iron, and Tin

Although the blacksmiths made all the iron cooking tools and utensils used by our ancestors in those early days, the tinsmiths are the ones who have been remembered longest, probably because more was written about them. One of the things made by them, certainly not the most intricate nor the most outstanding, but the one used by more people for a longer time, was the tin cup. The reason it is so well remembered is the fact one cup was shared by all the children in the country schools. Its community use did not stop there. It was used by all the farm hands working in the fields, whether related or not. When a bucket of cold water was taken to the field for everybody working there, there was only the one cup or dipper. Apparently there was no fear of spreading diseases. As late as 1960 it was not unusual to find a tin cup or dipper hanging near a spring in the mountains. It was there for the convenience of anyone who passed and was thirsty. Even in the home there was only one bucket of water and one cup or dipper, usually a dipper. The bucket of water would be brought from the spring or well and placed on the water shelf, either in the kitchen or on the back porch. This custom flourished for many years in the rural areas.

This fascination for and use of tinware began in 1738 when two brothers, William and Edgar Pattison, arrived from their native Ireland to set up shop in Berlin, Connecticut. The brothers were expert tinsmiths, having learned their trade in their homeland, and they are believed to be the first experienced tinsmiths to arrive in America. With their expertise it was only natural their tinwares were an instant success. It would be difficult today to say exactly what made them so successful, but there were probably several reasons. One would certainly be the expert workmanship, another could be the variety of pieces they made, and prices are said to have been very reasonable which would definitely have had a great bearing on their sales. It has also been recorded that in the beginning they were so anxious to please their customers they did small repairs and made pieces, on the spot, to fit the customer's needs.

Of course price had a lot to do with the popularity of the tinware, just as it always has, but there were other factors as well. When the Pattisons started making tinware, the majority of people who would buy the most tinware were using wooden trenchers or plates for meals and drinking their beverages from wooden mugs. China and glassware were known and used by some of the more affluent families, but it was much too expensive for the average families. China and glass were also easily broken which meant they were not very durable. Pewter was also available and at a lesser price, but it too had drawbacks, including the fact it was so soft it would bend easily. But the biggest drawback was the fact that if it was left too near the fire, pewter would melt. For the same reason, it could not be used on the woodburning stoves that came later.

The reputation of the Pattisons and their tinware grew, and soon they were loading baskets full of tinware on their horses, and venturing farther and farther from home as they searched for new customers. After a while they began to have competition as some of the young men who had served apprenticeships with the Pattisons had gone into business for themselves. They too were traveling all over New England looking for new business. Within a few decades the tinsmiths were buying horses and wagons, loading them with the tinwares they had made during the winter, and sending them into the southern and midwestern parts of the country. Some drove their own wagons while others hired drivers.

Once upon a time in America the homemaking ability of the housewife was judged by the number of fluffy feather beds she owned. At another time her abilities were judged by the number of shiny, new tin utensils she had. Happy was the bridegroom whose bride brought a dower chest filled with fine tinware. Later the bride would fill her dower chest with fine linens, most of which she had made herself, and they were as well received as the tin had been earlier.

A multitude of tin items continued to be made, until around 1850 when it seemed any cooking tool or utensil the cook could possibly need had been made in tin. By this time many of the tin eating and drinking utensils were being made of glass and china, but the demand for tin cooking utensils and accessories remained strong. Even today the demand for old tin remains strong, but now it is used more for decorating than for utilitarian purposes. Some tin items are still being made, probably because they are so collectible. With patience some of these new ones can be aged to look old. One example of this is the old fashioned, tin nutmeg graters, but care must be given when buying them today as new ones have been and still are being made in Mexico, maybe other places as well. Other tinware, quality tinware, is being made by hand by tinsmiths using the same type tools and methods as those used by the Pattisons. The same thing is happening with copper and brass. And here and there are blacksmiths who can hammer out fancy cooking tools and utensils when the spirit moves them. These workers sell from their shops while others sell at craft fairs and shows. They are made for people who may want to use them as they were used previously, or they might just want them to decorate their homes. One of the old pieces that is very collectible today, whether made by early or present day craftsmen, is the candle holder. Candle holders were made in a myriad of styles, and were made in all four materials — copper, brass, iron, and tin.

Copper tea kettle, porcelain handles, finial, and spout cover. $20-$25

Another tin item that is very collectible today is the bird roaster. It too is being reproduced, but in very limited numbers as far as is known. It is very popular among those trying to achieve a primitive look. Bird roasters are almost essential, if one has a fireplace and is trying to recreate an early kitchen. Originally they were designed and made to roast birds. First, it was bob whites, and later quail and doves. The dressed birds were hung on the hooks in the roaster, and placed in front of the fire where the birds roasted to a golden brown. Tin apple roaster are very similar, and were used the same way. Tin meat and turkey roasters were made along the same lines except there were no hook like in the bird roasters, nor shelves like in the apple roasters. A tin food warmer was also made that was similar to both except the majority of them were funnel-shaped. The warmer was used in front of the fire to warm the food from one meal to the next.

Cookie cutters, both the old and newer ones, are very popular in collecting circles. One of the reasons for that is the fact so many have Christmas designs or shapes, and nearly everybody bakes for the holidays. Cookie cutters of all kinds and ages can be found in most antique malls, shops, and flea markets. Some of the very late cookie cutters will be priced in the $3 range now.

Not surprising perhaps, tin was used to make horns, the noise making variety, in those early days when it was one of the cheapest and most plentiful of metals. Those horns were almost essential for the stage coach drivers. They used such horns to alert the innkeeper that they were on their way and would have so many guests for the next meal. The number of toots on the horn announced that many people would be wanting a meal. Those old horns will often be found now at old stagecoach inn restorations, especially in Georgia. Although it might be a bit shorter (about medium length) than the stagecoach horn, this same type horn was used on river boats plying the waters all over the country. When used on the boats they were needed to alert other boats of their approach, especially in foggy weather. A somewhat smaller tin horn was used on smaller boats that traveled along the rivers and the coast of New England.

Tin was a very important part of the lighting system in the early days. It was used to make candle molds to form the candles, and then it was used to make candle holders for those candles. Tin chandeliers were also popular. It is hard to find the early examples now, but newer ones have been and are still being made for those who want the appearance without too much worry about age. Later on oil lamps would be made of tin, but they were never too popular, apparently, as they are not nearly as plentiful as the glass oil lamps. It seems that quite a few of the tin oil lamps were made for use on the railroads. Most of them appears to have been bracket-type lamps that could be attached to the wall. This prevented them from tipping over on a table. Aladdin lamps were made in glass, brass, tin, and aluminum. They continue to be made with one of the later brass ones used in an illustration.

Tin bread trays have been in existence for a century or so, and some of those early one with floral decorations painted on can be very expensive today. In so many cases the early paintings have deteriorated with the many washing they have received. Some of these have been repainted – solid black. The tray is old, but the new paint job has taken away most of the antique value. Then there are others who have tried to paint a new floral design. This has not enhanced its value either. Old tin milk pans have gone through a similar experience. Although they never had a painted design, nevertheless flower loving people have tried to add a floral design later. Admittedly it has helped, because nobody wants an old rusty milk pan. With a floral decoration it does become a fair decorative addition to most kitchens.

Not everybody can find good examples of old, handmade tinware, and by the same token not everybody wants to. Lots of people prefer the later tinware, the pieces they remember from grandmother's house. But there is one rarity we would all like to find, especially lovers of kitchen antiques and collectibles, and that is the tin rolling pin. They are scarcer than the proverbial hen's tooth. During 10 years of diligent searching, they have evaded us completely. When questioned about them, several dealers have admitted they never heard of them. But they are a reality as one has been seen in a collection.

Equally as many pieces were made in brass and copper. Maybe more than in tin. So many of them are later pieces, but they are very attractive. They do not seem to be as collectible as the iron and tin, and it is possible this stems from the fact they have to be polished on a regular basis, if they are to continue to "shine." There are few things prettier than freshly polished brass and silver. The key word here is freshly: it has to be done so often. Few people have the time today to polish it regularly.

Copper was used to make all kinds of cookware. A copper canister set is shown. All of them are lined with tin as are most of the pots and pans.

Three large, copper skillets, tinned inside, brass handles, Philippe, La France trademark. $20-$30 each

Two medium-sized copper skillets, brass handles, tinned inside, unmarked. $15-$20 each

Large copper mixing bowl. $25-$30

Set of three graduated copper mixing bowls. $24-$28

71

Copper well and tree platter, probably silver plated originally, later stripped. $40-$45

Copper trivet, wooden handle. $13-$18

Late copper double boiler, top made of porcelain to protect the foods. $23-$26

Copper cooking kettle with chef's whisk. $40-$50

Four piece copper canister set, tinned inside. $35-$40 set

Brass bowl. $10-$12

Fancy brass tray. $25-$30

Brass cup. $8-$10

Old brass candle holder. $18-$22

Small, heavy, brass container. $18-$22

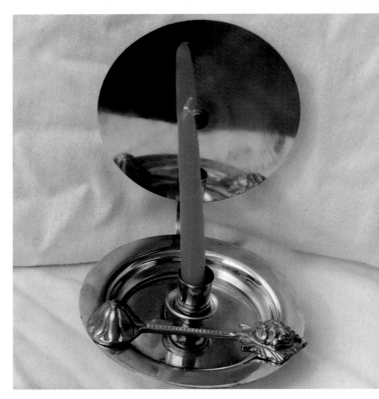

Brass candle holder with shield and brass candle snuffer. Candle holder $24-$28, snuffer $18-$22

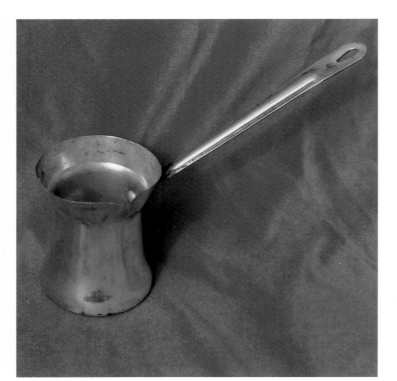

Long handled brass cup or measure. $10-$12

Late Aladdin oil lamp in brass with green shade. $60-$75

Hanging match holder for early 5 cent boxes of kitchen matches, reproduction, but attractive. $7-$9

Iron mold for hogshead cheese. Made in the shape of a hog's head. $100-$125

Blacksmith-made, iron Hole and Peg trammel for cooking in the fireplace a couple of centuries ago. $95-$125

Iron Dutch oven could be hung on trammel or banked with hot coals for cooking, unmarked. $25-$35

Owl andirons, circa 1925. $300-$350

Close-up of the handles of the owl fireplace tools.

Owl fireplace tools to match the owl andirons. $100-$150

Late iron cookie pan decorated with animals. $12-$15

Old tin cups like this one were hung on well posts or by the spring house. $7-$9

Tin lady finger pan. $10-$12

Tin roaster for roasting birds in front of the fireplace. $50-$75

Tin strainer for straining milk into large cans. $10-$12

Early tin container. $25-$30

Painted, tin match box. Later than the iron ones. $5-$9

Old tin milk pan decorated later with floral designs. $18-$30 depending on the quality of the paintings

Late, hand made, tin, hanging candle holder. $8-$10

Late tin cup. Circa 1930-40. $5-$7

Tin picnic basket, wooden handles. $22-$28

Small tin bucket. Used as a lunch pail by school children in the late 1800s. $18-$25

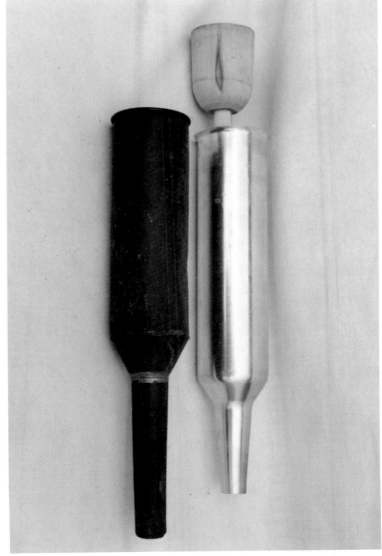

Old tin sausage stuffer with later aluminum one. Tin $15-$18, Aluminum $9-12

Chapter Eight
Egg Utensils

Our ancestors were a frugal lot, well maybe not frugal from choice as much as from the fact they were cash poor. The only time the farmer had cash was when he sold his crops in the fall, and in those days they didn't get big prices. That money had to last them for a year. Still they were not much different from the people living in the towns and villages who might have a business or a job, but whose profits or salaries would probably amount to about one percent of what people make today. Therefore they had to be frugal, and raise as much of their food as possible. One of the easiest things to raise was chickens. The eggs they produced were an extra bonus, and both could be enjoyed year round. Extra eggs could be set, that is the hen could be allowed to sit on the eggs in a nest for about three weeks — until chicks were hatched. Although the family came first and eggs were always saved for their use, surplus eggs were sold or bartered for other foods. The excess chickens were either eaten or sold.

Therein lies one of the greatest stories of the past as well as the present because the egg and the utensils used with it are more popular today than they were originally. That lowly little egg has been responsible for as many, if not more antiques and collectibles than any other single item in "antiquedom." It goes from the lowly egg beater that is now enjoying so much popularity to the very elegant Fabergé eggs. Goldsmith Peter Carl Fabergé made fifty three fabulous eggs, eggs made of gold and precious stones. Originally they were made for the Russian Czar Nicholas III who gave them to his wife Czarina Maria Feodorovna as gifts. Today those eggs whose whereabouts are known are either in museums or private collection. When they go on the market, which is very seldom, they sell for hundreds of thousands of dollars. That leaves the ordinary egg collectibles for the average collector.

But that shouldn't worry collectors as there are multitudes of choice, reasonably-priced, egg-related antiques just waiting to be found. One of the better known, with the exception of the egg beater and about as plentiful, is the egg basket. Until a few decades ago every farm home had at least two egg baskets, often more. One was used for gathering the eggs while the other was used for taking the surplus eggs to the store for "trading." In the meantime, if the family had large flocks of hens and they were producing lots of eggs, they had to have yet another basket, this one for storing eggs until they were eaten or sold. Not all egg baskets were alike. Some areas preferred one style while others preferred another. In the northeast they didn't seem to have had as many egg baskets as other parts of the country so it is difficult to say one particular style was the favorite. But in the south two styles were favored, the round or the oblong. Now in the middle or mountain states the buttocks baskets became the accepted egg baskets.

The egg has become so closely related to Easter it would be impossible to think of it without eggs. Perhaps in its own way this is in relation to the Roman proverb: All life comes from an egg. When the relationship between Easter and the egg began is unknown, but it is known that Easter is the time for egg hunts, egg rolls, and it is the time when the Easter Bunny brings baskets laden with bright colored eggs. Today there are more chocolate eggs in the Easter baskets than boiled and dyed hen's eggs, but they are eggs nevertheless.

Years ago the housewife gave little thought to eggs except to be sure she had enough for the family's use. She might have a slight interest in the price of eggs, that is, what the grocer would pay her for the surplus eggs. Then about a century ago things began to change. Now the buyer was concerned about the size of the eggs. They wanted them uniform in size. For example, they wanted either all large or all small eggs, not mixed sizes. And they wanted to know they were all fresh. To solve the first problem they began inventing egg scales. Several types were made and all seemed to have been popular. With that problem solved, the inventors turned their attention to ways to check for the freshness of the eggs. They soon came up with egg candlers, the first being a round, tin container with a window on one side. The egg lay in a cup-shaped container on top and the light from the window on the side was supposed to enable the owner to look through the egg and see if it was fresh or not. Strangely enough it worked fairly well considering there had been nothing before. But when compared to present day egg testing it leaves much to be desired. Both the scales and candlers are quite collectible today.

The country store owner who bought or bartered for all the extra eggs in his community had to find ways to dispose of them. It wasn't an easy chore when all the people in his area had chickens. But the store owners soon devised ways to dispose of the extras — they shipped them by train to the city where large store owners were delighted to get them. Whereas nearly everybody in the rural areas had chickens, few in the cities had them. In the early days it was different, but as the cities became more settled the raising of livestock and chickens was left for the farm families.

Shipping the eggs created the need for a container, so somebody invented a tin box or crate that would hold twelve dozen eggs. According to the son of one early East Tennessee storekeeper, a grocer might have as many as six or eight of these crates ready for shipping when the train made its weekly trip. That gives us an idea how many eggs were produced at that time, if they had that many more than the families could use.

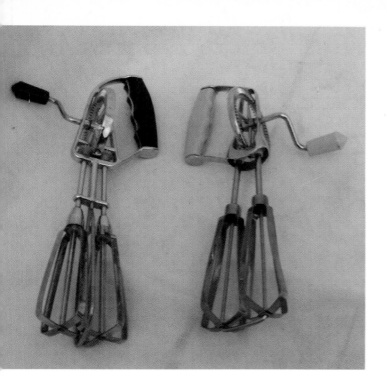

Two late egg beaters. $7-$9 each

When and where the housewife first discovered how to separate the eggs using the yolks for pies and cakes, and the whites for frosting is unknown, but discover it they did. Some of the early housewives used a fork to beat the whites to a frothy icing, then someone discovered an egg beater and it did the job better. That was a period when everybody seemed to have an idea for making everything more useful, thereby making life easier. The egg beaters took many forms before they settled for the rotary, and even that was made in a variety of styles by a large group of manufacturers which accounts for the large number still available today. The next step for the egg beater was to electrify it so that it became known as an electric mixer and was used for everything including beating eggs.

Long before the egg beater there was the egg cup. A soft boiled egg or two was a favorite for breakfast for a century or more. In fact, soft boiled eggs were more of a favorite then than cereal is now. The popularity of the soft boiled egg seems to have begun during the Victorian era, and if those ladies didn't do anything else, they served food correctly. Therefore they didn't just serve a boiled egg; they served it in an egg cup. Fifty years ago it was next to impossible to find a set of dishes, Haviland or otherwise, that didn't include egg cups. Then as now there were collectors who only collected egg cups which probably explains some of the shortage, but there are still enough to keep collectors happy and searching. Unfortunately the egg cup seems to be more popular today for its "collectibility" than for its usefulness.

A wire gadget that was and still is closely associated with the egg is one usually referred to as an egg separator. It can be used to separate the whites from the yolks, or to remove boiled eggs from hot water. Reports are it has also been used to beat egg whites (for icing) when nothing else was available.

One egg related item that was once thought to be extremely scarce has proved during the last half dozen years to be rather plentiful, at least in some areas, and that item is the so-called Egg Cooker. This assumption of scarcity was based on the fact that one was seldom seen a few years ago, yet today it is

not unusual to see one in at least one booth at some antique malls. So far they don't seem to be extremely popular because the same ones will remain on the same shelves for a long time. Price could be a factor as most are priced from around $35 to $65. The lower priced ones are generally the later ones made in Japan. Earlier they were priced higher, but lack of sales could have driven prices down. They were first made around 1921 by the Hankscraft Company, Madison, Wisconsin. They are simply little, round bowls with an insert that holds up to four eggs. A round, domed lid fits over the top. Directions are given on the bottom as to just how to cook them. One of the things that made them so popular in the Forties and Fifties, other than the fact people ate so many boiled eggs, was the variety of colors in which they were made — colors that matched the new and very popular Fiesta dinnerware.

For centuries the egg has remained a very popular food. It has remained popular probably because eggs were and still are prepared in so many ways and used in so many dishes. Maybe before, but certainly during the Thirties through the Fifties poached seems to have been one of the more popular ways to prepare eggs. This is partly based on the variety of tools and utensils made especially for poaching eggs. Since large families were the norm they needed lots of eggs. The smaller family only needed a few so the two egg poacher was developed. It was called a Poacherette. However the majority appears to have had spaces for four eggs with some being round, others square. The shapes apparently added variety to the breakfast menu. Some of the egg poachers look like little stoves with a space in the bottom for other foods while a pan above that held water for the eggs.

Not only were eggs dyed and used at Easter, they were used in other ways. One of those ways was decoration, and one that is most attractive is the Cloisonne egg. Cloisonne is one of the oldest types of enameling, and it has been used to make all types of things including an egg-shaped piece. Another way, a very inexpensive way, was very popular about 25 years ago. A whole but empty egg shell was obtained either by preparing it at home, or buying it at a craft shop. It was then painted with some attractive design. Moss was put into a new whisk, the egg was put on the moss so that it looked like an egg in a nest, and bows of fabric ribbon were tied around the handle. These ornaments were made and hung in one's own kitchen, or they might be given to a friend to use in her kitchen.

Egg Poacherette. $7-$9

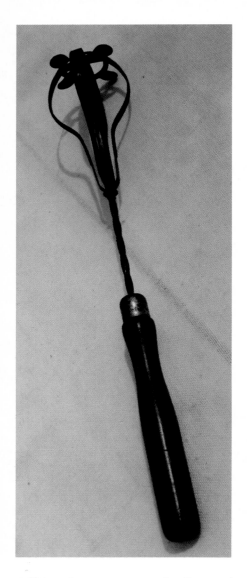

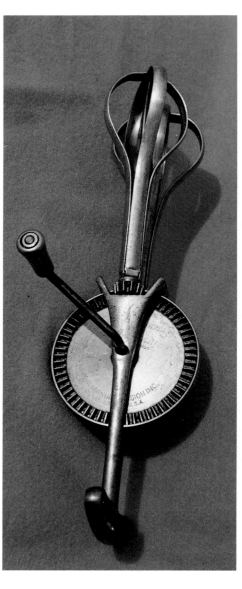

Old egg beater, pressure on handle caused bottom to rotate. $20-$25

Stainless steel egg beater, A&J in diamond trademark. $20-$25

Aluminum Beauty egg beater, pat'd April 20, 1920, made by Ullman Aluminum Division, Inc., Long Island City, New York. $24-$30

China egg cup. $15-$18

Late electric egg cooker with rooster design. $29-$35

Glass bottoms on electric egg beaters break easily. A modern crockery jar can be used to replaced the broken glass bottom. Beaters alone can be found for as little as $5 or less, crockery jars for $3-$5.

When assembled the beater is both attractive and useful.

About 25 years ago this craft project of combining a painted egg shell, moss, whisk, and ribbon made a nice kitchen decoration. $5-$8

Late colorful, Cloisonne egg. $25-$50

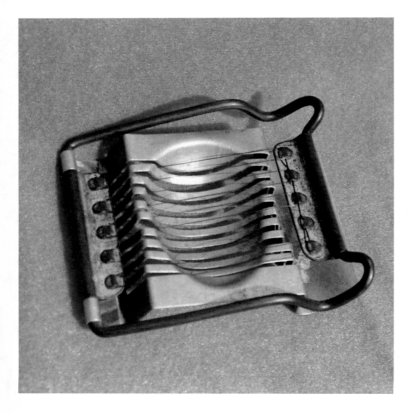

Egg slicer for boiled eggs. $5-$7

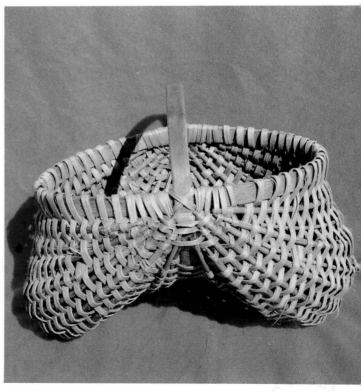

Splint, buttocks egg basket, not the best workmanship. $20-$25

Egg slicer for slicing eggs vertically. $13-$18

Oak splint egg basket, favorite in the south. $35-$40

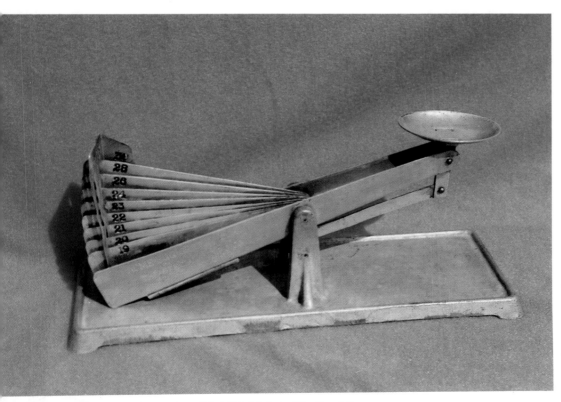

Acme Egg Grading Scale, pat. June 24, 1924. Made by The Specialty
Manufacturing Company, St. Paul, Minnesota. $30-$35

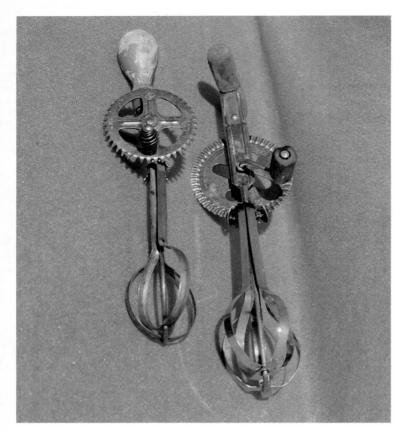

Two rotary egg beaters. One with worn green handle has patent date October 9, 1923. $14-$18. High Speed Super Center Drive Beater, Ekco, handles never painted. $18-$23

Pan for poaching eggs, round spaces, unmarked. $12-$14

Pan for poaching eggs, square spaces. Merit Aluminum trademark. $15-$18

Kenmor electric egg beater with a heavy glass bottom. $20-$30

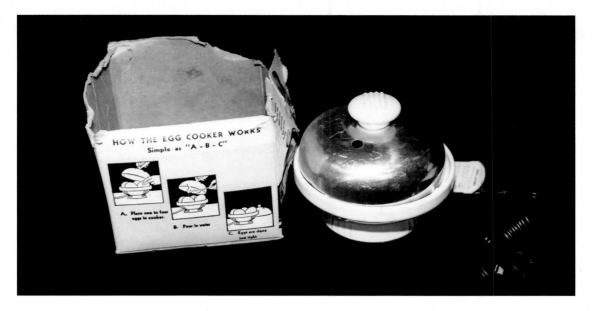

Electric egg cooker with original box. $19-$35

Super Whirl egg beater, yellow handles, made by The Turner and Seymour Manufacturing Company, Torrington, Connecticut. $20-$28

Old egg separator. $10-$12

Ekco egg beater, hand operated, with glass bottom. $15-$22

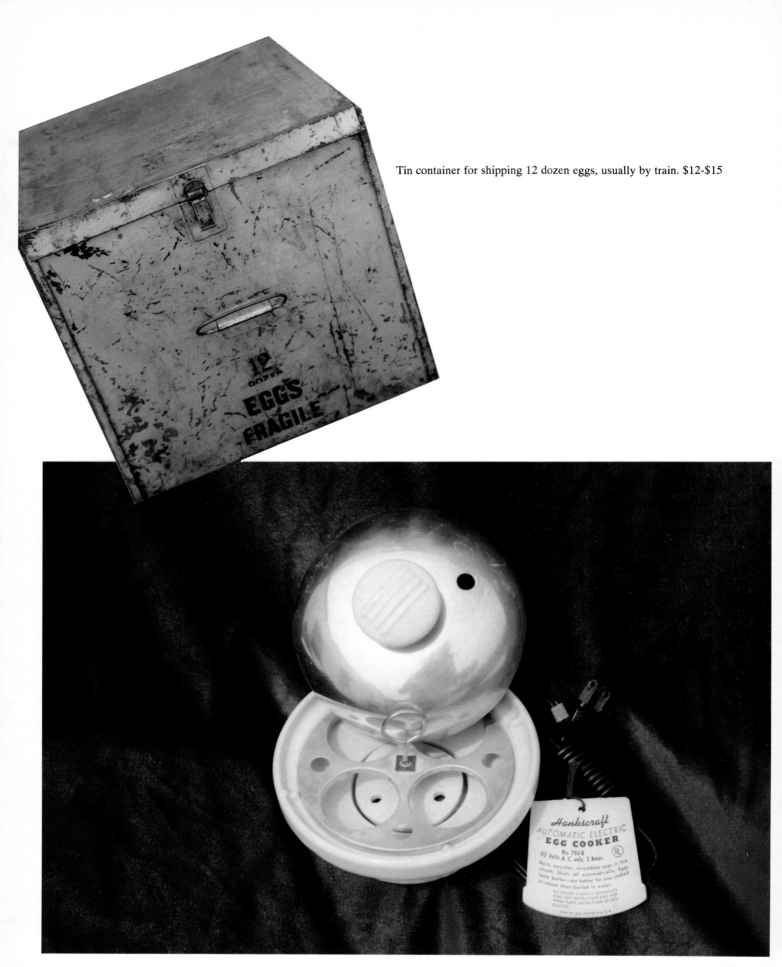

Tin container for shipping 12 dozen eggs, usually by train. $12-$15

Hankscraft electric egg cooker, directions still attached to the cord.
$29-$39

Chapter Nine
Graniteware

It has been said that enameling is older than history, yet new as tomorrow. That is probably true as the production of enameling may have slowed from time to time, but it has never stopped completely. As early as the 15th century man was producing enameling in one form or another. If any enameled housewares were made at that time, no records have been found. It is doubtful anyone has really looked for records of housewares from that time for several reasons. One reason was the fact that utensils and housewares were not that plentiful, nor that widely used early on. Another reason could be that fancy cookery was not being done then. Reports are cooking was rather crude even into the 17th and 18th centuries although some countries like France were well known for their fine foods. It all depends on where you look as to what information you will find, but chances are most of the affluent in all countries dined on well prepared food, although the tools and utensils used to prepare it might seem crude by today's standards. It is known that a lot of decorative enameling was being done as early as the 15th century. This included cloisonne, champleve, bassetaille, pique-a-jour, and emaux peints. The last was a painted enamel that could have later been varied to produce the graniteware cooking utensils and housewares that are so avidly sought today. But with all the popularity of graniteware cooking utensils we still have to admit it is a poor relation of the finer enamels.

Other than the fine enamels, most of the others can be lumped under the heading of porcelain enamels. The term porcelain enamel covers everything from enameled store fronts to graniteware cooking utensils. Until a century or so ago enameling was classed as one of the fine arts, then someone gave it a practical twist by applying it to cast iron pots and pans. When it was found the coat of enamel made them safer, easier to clean, and much prettier, they went on to enameling bigger things like the old woodburning, iron cook stove.

We have to recognize graniteware as one of the kitchen tools and utensils with staying power when we remember it has enchanted housewives for well over a century. Those first homemakers were tired of black iron pots and pans and welcomed the colorful pieces of graniteware. Anything to lighten their load of household chores, with cooking leading the list. So the first ones bought it to use while today's collectors buy it primarily to display and to decorate their homes, although some graniteware collectors use their pieces regularly.

Today we tend to use the one term, graniteware, as an umbrella to cover all types of enameled cookware. That was not the custom years ago. Around the turn of the present century it was simply called Enameled Ware, then Agate or Agate Ironware, and finally Swirl. One company advertised their product under the name "Royal Gray Granite Enameled Steel Ware." That name made it perfectly clear what it was and how it was made.

In 1878 the firm of Lalance and Grosjean, a manufacturing company located in New York, exhibited some of their enameled wares at the Paris Exposition and won the coveted Grand Gold Medal. Apparently this was the boost the company needed as 8 years later they were distributing a catalog of over 100 pages devoted entirely to their graniteware cooking utensils. Other than the white and gray that was so commonly used then, they are believed to have been the first to introduce blue and white graniteware utensils, with the big mottled design. Lalance and Grosjean were not the only ones making graniteware at that time because it was just about that time that Butler Brothers, a wholesaler rather than a manufacturer, was offering coffee pots, the two quart size, for $9 a dozen; tea pots in the same size at the same price; five quart sauce pans were $7.50 a dozen; the same size preserving kettles were the same price; five quart tea kettles were $17.10 a dozen; fry pans or skillets were $4.40 a dozen while plates could be bought for $1.80 a dozen. These pieces seem unusually cheap, but graniteware was cheap in those days. Another reason for these cheap prices is the fact they are wholesale prices, and the retailer would have to add a little profit. Graniteware prices stayed very reasonable until around 25 years ago when it became so collectible. Prices rose along with its popularity. Back in those early days Butler Brothers described those pieces mentioned above as "Only a few of the more common household articles made in Agate Ironware." Gray was the most popular color in those early days, and still is with some collectors. At that time gray was described as having the "the peculiar appearance of mottled stone." The biggest selling point for graniteware then was the fact it was lined with enamel making it as easy to clean as crockery. Many people liked that feature while others seemed to just love the colorful enamel.

Graniteware became so popular it began to be made by numerous companies and made in a rainbow of colors. One of the reasons for its popularity was that it fit the needs of so many segments of our society. A couple of decades or so after the end of the Civil War it began to be made in such quantities one could almost say it was mass produced. During this time covered wagons rumbling westward were being outfitted with graniteware cooking utensils because they was tough enough to stand the trip, outfitters said. Graniteware also jangled from the hooks inside the chuck wagons as they followed the drovers up and down the cattle trails of the west. Anyone who loves western movies is familiar with the lonely cowboy making coffee in his graniteware coffee pot after his day's work is done. In the movies as well as in real life, probably, he often made coffee in the morning before starting work. Western movies alone have probably introduced more people to the use of graniteware than any other one thing. The same movies show how the railroad crews depended on graniteware cooking utensils, especially the coffee pots and mugs, as they laid the rails that now crisscross the country.

The west wasn't the only place where graniteware earned its stripes. It was used profusely in the kitchens of the Army. Navy, and Marines. The chuck wagon cooks had proved how durable it was, so during World War I military cooks continued the tradition. They found it especially useful and durable in field kitchens. Maybe it was the returning military cooks who introduced graniteware into prisons where it was used for decades, both for cooking and for serving. Records show that it was also popular in the old "poor farms" as well as most mental institutions. It has been found that at that time government (city, county, and state) was one of the biggest purchasers of graniteware. As far as can be determined they only bought white, no colors. That would seem logical as the white looked more sanitary.

Graniteware was so widely used from 1910 through 1930 that it would be hard to find a hospital or a doctor's office that was not outfitted then with white graniteware, everything from a mortar and pestle to a sterilizer. The demand for these old medical pieces is not great, nor do we know one collector at present who is interested. But there have been a few through the years.

For three quarters of a century, from around 1875 to 1950, there was hardly a person alive who was not affected in some way by the use of graniteware. It was used by the rich as well as the poor, by the famous and the infamous. It could be found in every kitchen from the socialite's to the mountaineer's. No other one item crossed the country as many times or on as many types of transportation — horseback, wagon, and train.

If you decide to collect graniteware and want the old, it behooves novice collectors to learn early the difference between the old and that made in Mexico and other countries during the past two or three decades. Some of the new was mixed with the old during the early days of the new, and it has aged making it very difficult to tell one from the other. Many of the old pieces had trademarks that have lasted as they were stamped on; others had paper labels that were lost in the sink long ago. Unless a piece of graniteware has the trademark of the manufacturer, not the trademark of the wholesaler or retailer, it is next to impossible to trace it to its maker. Many large wholesale houses that either made some of their products or had them made especially for the company used various names to identify pieces or colors. For example, Norvell-Shapleigh Hardware Company used different trademarks for each color, Shamrock Ware was used on green, Blue Diamond was for blue and white mottled, Dixie for blue and white speckled, and White Diamond for white graniteware.

Gray graniteware coffee pot with matching stove. $300-$500

Two blue and white graniteware water kettles. $150-$200 each

Damaged blue and white graniteware flask. Most found today will have some damage. $200-$750 depending on the amount of damage

Blue and white graniteware lunch pail or lunch carrier. $175-$250

Teapot described in an early book as relish-colored graniteware. $175-$225

An assortment of graniteware in assorted colors from a red soap dish on the top shelf to a yellow and white mottled water kettle on the bottom.

Turk's Head cake pan or mold. Red graniteware outside, gray inside. $150-$250

Assortment of blue and white graniteware pots, some without lids.
Prices can ranged from $95 for the two on the left without lids to $300
for the small teapot on the right.

Blue and white graniteware milk cans in sizes from one pint to one
half gallon. Pint size $185-$215, quart size $175-$200, half gallon
size $165-$185

Blue and white graniteware bowl
and pitcher, rare. $250-$400

93

GRANITE IRON WARE IS "ALL THE GOSSIP"

Major, Knapp & Co. 56 & 58 Park Place N.Y.

PATENT
GRANITE IRON WARE

THE GOSSIPS.
The picture on the other side of this card represents a tea-party of experienced house-keepers discussing the merits of the GRANITE IRON WARE.

This scene is of frequent occurrence wherever these wares are in use. It is not gossip, however, to say that the GRANITE IRON WARE is without a peer, and its growing popularity is such that no home is thoroughly equipped without a full supply of these wares. If you are in favor of cleanliness, healthfulness and economy, use the GRANITE IRON WARE.
"A word to the wise is sufficient."

DEAN & COMPANY,
ANN ARBOR, MICH.

Front of trade card advertising Granite Iron Ware, one of the early names for graniteware. $25-$30

Back of trade card.

Unusual white graniteware hot plate. $30-$50

Granite Iron Ware trade card showing graniteware milk bucket. $25-$30

Granite Iron Ware trade card introducing "The little Housewife," or showing how the young girls were learning to use cooking utensils. $25-$30

Back of trade card.

Heavy gray graniteware roaster. $30-$40

Red graniteware coffee pot. $75-$95

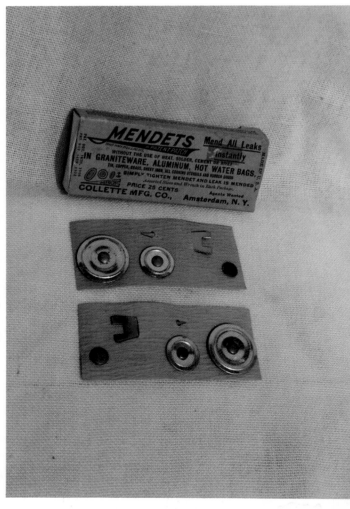

Mendets were popular for repairing tin, but reached their peak of popularity mending holes in graniteware. $5-$7 box

Blue and white speckled graniteware over iron roaster. L. L. Bean trademark. $40-$45

Two small graniteware roasters, late. $15-$20 each

Late, yellow graniteware coffee pot. $10-$15

Chapter Ten
Graters, Grinders, Cutters, Choppers, and Crackers

Many items in this category range from early examples that more often than not were handmade to the later factory-made items. The handmade examples were usually limited to one, maybe two, per family. The homemaker usually had a preference for one specific tool that she used on a regular basis. She might acquire others, but most of the time she remained faithful to the one she liked best. Actually the men weren't all that anxious to make new tools so it wasn't until factory models were made that she allowed herself the luxury of several tools of the same kind like biscuit cutters. In the early days, the husband made wooden biscuit cutters, then the tinsmith began making tin ones, and finally factories were turning out carloads of both tin and aluminum biscuit cutters for prices of 3 to 5 cents each. And if they did not object to advertising on their biscuit cutters, they could get free ones from flour companies as well as baking powder companies.

The story of the cookie cutter borders on that of the biscuit cutter. About the only difference was the fact the biscuit cutter was used everyday, sometimes twice a day, while the cookie cutters might only be used once or twice a week. That meant the biscuit cutter was more important, therefore more were needed. The doughnut cutter was about as important as the cookie cutter, although that would depend on the individual families. One might prefer cookies over doughnuts while another family would reverse the preference. Bakeries were not too plentiful, even fifty years ago, so most cookies and doughnuts were cooked at home. This in turn helps to explain the wide variety of cutters still available to the collector. Of course the cutters are still being made, but the majority found in stores today are made of plastic. Tin ones will be seen from time to time in specialty stores — displayed side by side with the plastic ones. One of the reasons for the popularity of the older models is the fact so many housewives want to encourage nostalgia at Christmas by making cookies cut with the old cutters. So many of the older ones have a very pronounced Christmas design which makes the chore easy.

Many people have herb gardens today, but a century ago it would have been next to impossible to find a home that did not have one. The thought of buying prepared herbs probably never crossed their minds. The housewife gathered her own, dried them, and ground them to her specifications. For some things she could use a mortar and pestle, likely homemade by her husband, but for others she needed a special tool, this one also handmade by her husband. The style and quality of the tool depended on the skill of the husband and the desires of the wife.

The first all-purpose herb grinder was a sort of trough with a roller that could be moved from one end to the other by hand. Iron versions of this one was also made by the blacksmith. Both of these are scarce now. A supposed improvement on this type was produced by making a round, wooden masher type that could be rolled around in a bowl to crush the herbs. The wooden masher was made in several styles that could be used with either a wooden or stoneware bowl. Then there were the tin nutmeg graters and later the Mouli graters that were indispensable to the housewives.

Pepper was another seasoning that required its own mill. It wasn't homegrown, instead it was bought whole and ground at home. No doubt it was ground earlier in a mortar and pestle, but it too eventually acquired its own mill. These mills have been seen made of wood, brass, glass, and tin as well as the later plastic ones.

The plastic ones are not old enough to be collectible yet. Coffee mills are also quite collectible now, but the good ones, those made of tin, wood, iron, glass, and china are scarce while reproductions are plentiful. In those days the coffee beans were bought green, roasted at home in the oven, then ground in the coffee mill.

Those of us who grew up in the middle or southern sections of the country think of ice as a rather late addition to the needs of the household. But it was a staple in the northeast, especially in the state of Maine where it was harvested in winter and shipped south in sailing ships. People used saws to cut the ice into blocks, then it was stored in ice houses to await the arrival of another ship. The cooler temperatures of Maine helped to save the ice, but the icemen went a step further by building ice houses, usually a sort of cellar, sturdily built, in a hillside. The ice was packed in sawdust on the ships, and was usually taken to one of the southern islands where it was exchanged for rum that could be brought back and sold.

The types of tools used to break or crush the ice blocks are unknown. Later there would be ice shaves, ice crushers, and by the time ice became available to the masses there would be ice picks in a number of styles, many given away free because of the advertisement on the handle. Later small aluminum ice crushers that fit a cube or two of refrigerator-made ice became available. But before those were made there was an iron on a wooden base ice crusher complete with a handle that turned to crush the ice between the revolving teeth. These date from the 1920s and were very popular with people who made their own ice cream. This contraption made it easy to crush the 50 to 100 pound block of ice after it had been cut into smaller pieces. These blocks of ice might be delivered to the home by the iceman, or they could be obtained at the ice plant.

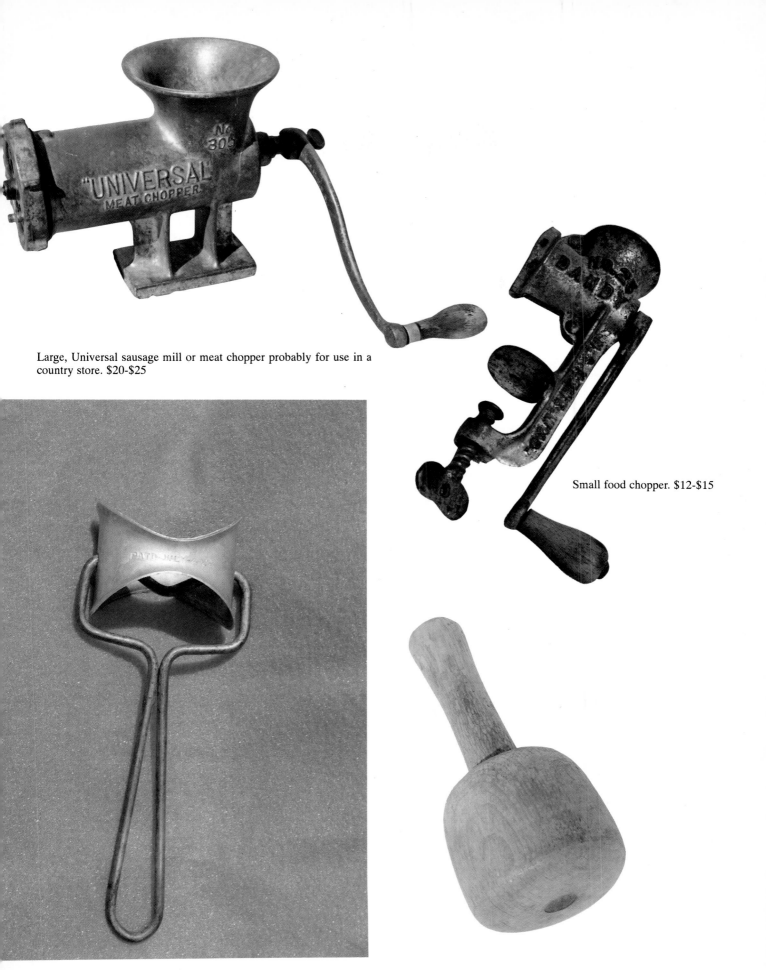

Large, Universal sausage mill or meat chopper probably for use in a country store. $20-$25

Small food chopper. $12-$15

Rolling biscuit cutter, Pat'd. July 4, 1922. Some will be found with advertising. $15-$18

Heavy, homemade herb grinder, probably used for other chores as well. $18-$20

Chandler's Ice Cutting Machine made by C. E. Jennings and Company, New York, Pat. November 18, 1890. $50-$75

Food chopper with 1.5 cup glass holder, red handle, only mark Pamco. $18-$20

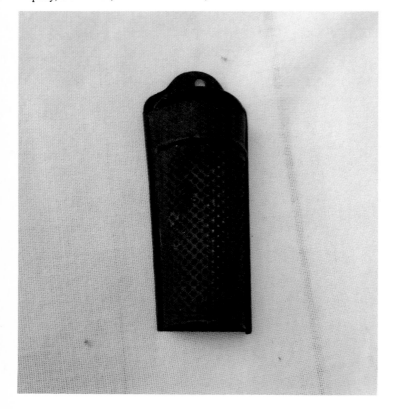

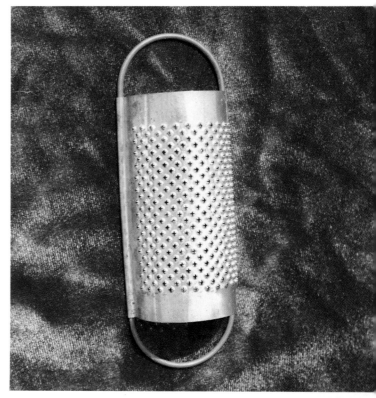

Old, well aged, tin nutmeg grater. $12-$15

Late tin nutmeg grater. $6-$8

Tin biscuit cutter and a doughnut cutter. $12-$15 each

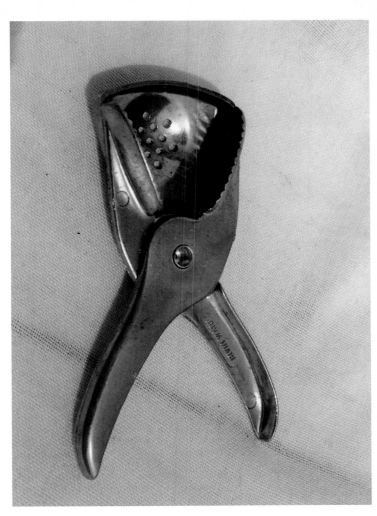

Metal lemon or lime squeezer. $8-$10

Chopping knife, especially good when chopping nuts. $8-$10

Garlic press. $6-$8

Two-blade chopping knife in a round wooden bowl. Knife 20-$24, late bowl $18-$20

Peanuts are put into the figure's mouth and the two handles pushed together to crack the nuts. $10-$12

Homemade horse radish grater. Since they were homemade, chances are slim collectors will ever find two exactly alike. $75-$100

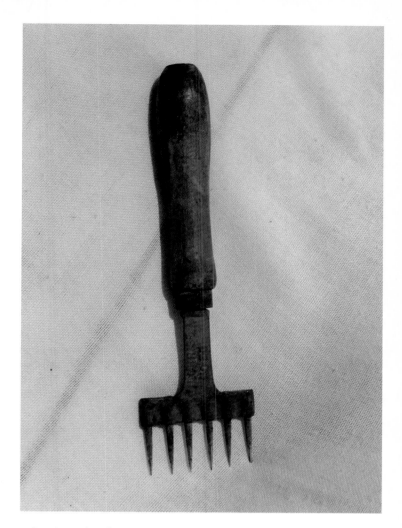

At one time or another every home in America has had one of these Four-in-One graters. Old ones are being painted or decorated with designs to add to the kitchen decor. $5-$7

Ice shave. $15-$17

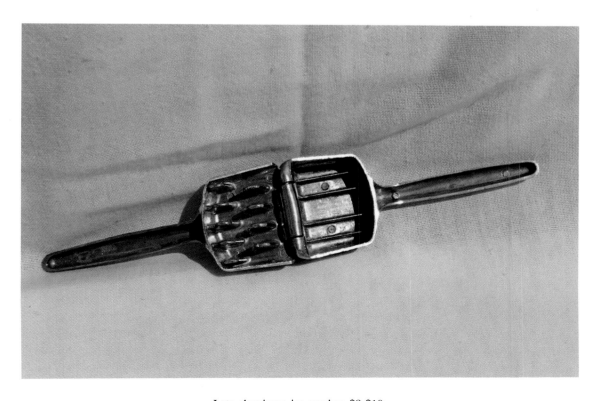

Late aluminum ice crusher. $8-$10

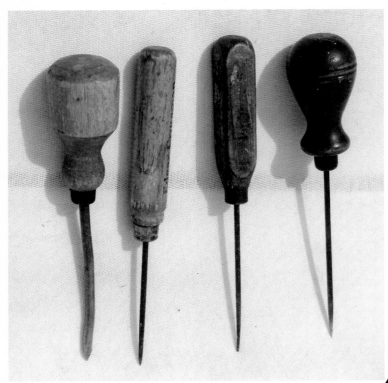

Four assorted ice picks ranging from early one on left to the advertising examples in the middle. $9-$15 each

Wooden lemon squeezer, circa 1900. $45-$60

Nut cracker used more for pecans down south. $20-$25

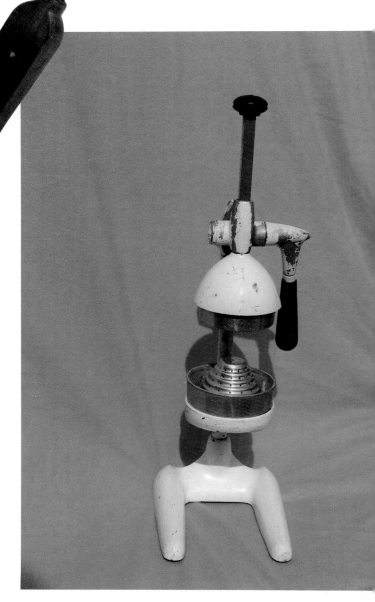

Juicer with hand crank. $18-$24

Heavy, homemade, wooden grinder — as useful for herbs as for grinding cornmeal. $24-$28

Homemade cutter, handy for cutting vegetables or tobacco. $50-75

Handmade brass pepper mill. $17-$21

Chapter Eleven
Iron on Tuesday

Once upon a time it was said that man worked from sun to sun, but woman's work was never done. This concept could have originated with the washing and ironing of clothes and household linens. They might not have had an excess of clothing and maybe only one set of sheets for each bed which does not sound bad when explained that way, but the problem arises when one realizes how many beds they had to have, and how many people were in each family. Big families were the norm for many years, in fact it was not unusual for farm families to have a dozen or more children born so close together they were all at home at the same time. We once knew a mountain man who had twenty one children — by three wives. Washing and ironing for that family must have been mind-boggling.

The washing was bad, but the ironing was worse because in summer a fire had to be kept in the fireplace or in the woodburning cook stove so the irons could be kept hot. It was not unusual to see rural women still using old sad irons that had to be heated on the stove as late as the Fifties. They had to use them as electricity was not available to many households prior to that time.

Those old sad irons are quite the collectibles now, but not to be used as they once were. Today they are used mostly for decorative purposes. Some may have been saved from an ancestor's home and kept simply for nostalgia while others are used to complete a collection of all types of irons. Some are painted a solid color and used as doorstops or bookends. Occasionally a person with some artistic talent will acquire the irons and after painting them add a design. Some are rather attractive. Some of the sad irons are really old, having been made by the local blacksmith while others are factory-made. Both types are very attractive, it all depends on what the collector prefers. Prices have edged up considerably during the last decade, but they still are not scarce as many families had dozens of sad irons. Since they were made of iron they had lasting power.

Then there were different irons for different chores like the sleeve irons used exclusively for ironing special types of sleeves. Another iron that was and still is unusual is the so-called tailor's goose, a heavy iron weighing around 16 to 18 pounds that was used by tailors, hence the name. It was bought and used occasionally by housewives, especially those who made woolen clothes for their families. The heavier iron was necessary when trying to iron the seams flat on woolen garments.

Actually there was more to ironing than just smoothing out wrinkles. Many of the clothes had to be starched to keep their fresh look. The starching idea seems to have originated with the ruff which in the beginning was simply a cotton collar with gophered edges. The trouble began as more and more collars were added until it became one of the most elaborate pieces of neckwear ever concocted. It was so elaborate it was next to impossible to keep it clean, and when it had to be washed and ironed, although the work was probably done by servants, it became an unforgettable experience. Keeping it washed and ironed was such a chore that when the style changed no one has ever tried to revive the ruff.

But the ruff can be credited with the creation of ruff starch, the forerunner of all the later starches, and the invention of the ruff iron. The details of the origin of starch like that of the iron has been lost in the mists of antiquity. Pliny mentioned a wheat starch being made during the first century, but whether it was suitable for clothing or not is unknown. It is known that by the 16th century ruff starch was available, but the price was so high only nobility and the very rich could afford it. Whether the high price was justified is unknown. It seems that in those days anything new and outstanding was priced out of reach for the masses. Perhaps the prices were inflated to assure only the very rich could afford the unusual things – that the person wearing a ruff would not be mistaken for a farmer in a handwoven shirt. Shortly thereafter, starch for use on ruffs began to be made from potatoes, and with potatoes so plentiful the price of the starch should have dropped, but no record of that could be found.

Records show that the early American settlers used potatoes to make their first starch. Later they would use wheat flour, and still later it would be white flour. In fact, as late as the 1940s there were women in the south who could pour a kettle of boiling water over a cup of white flour and make the finest starch. Some would add a few drops of kerosene to the starch and when cheap gingham dresses were starched in it and ironed, they looked like expensive polished cotton or chintz fabrics. Factory-made starches were available at that time, but it was hard for some women to break the old habit of making their own. And too they were not that far removed from their "Waste Not-Want Not" ancestors.

Factory-made starch had actually been available since around 1807 when two brothers, John and Edward Gilbert, built the first starch making factory in Utica, New York. They prospered, but it took a man named Thomas Kingsford to discover that starch could be made from corn which made it much cheaper.

There are those who think wrinkle-free clothes have been popular for only a couple of centuries while others think it has been much longer. The latter based their theory on reports that the 10th century, warring Vikings wanted their clothes to

Trivet for iron, metal on slate, marked Simplex. $12-$15

be wrinkle free. It is believed to have been around this time that pleated clothing became popular which meant another type of iron was necessary. So someone invented the so-called rocker iron, one with a round or rocker base. They were described as the type that could be heated and then rocked back and forth to "set" the pleats.

That was only the beginning. More and more irons began to be invented; each it seemed was an improvement over the last. There was the Mrs. Potts' type that was certainly an improvement over the single handle sad iron as the Potts' iron had one wooden handle that could be used on three bases. Two bases could be heating while the third was being used. There were several types of the so-called box iron. A heated lug or hot coals could be used in it despite the fact some people disagree with the hot coal use. This writer has seen both used in box irons therefore knows they will work. One of the advantages of this and other similar irons is the fact they didn't have to be heated in a fireplace or on the stove. For that reason they didn't have to contend with the soot and ashes associated with other types of irons, especially sad irons.

Two types of gas irons, one that worked off the natural gas line and one that used gasoline, were introduced. Both were an improvement over irons made previously. Perhaps the greatest improvement provided by the gas iron was that there was no need to keep a fire burning all day just to heat the irons which made this type ironing a much cooler chore.

On June 8, 1882 a New Yorker named Henry W. Weely received a patent for an electric iron. It is believed to have been the first one, but it certainly was not the last. Like all new inventions this one had problems. In this case the problem was lack of electricity to operate it. At that time electricity just was not available except in the larger cities and then only at night. The power companies were striving to furnish lights for the homes, and then only at night. They were not too concerned about the electrical appliances that had not yet been invented.

Believe it or not, the old adage "Iron on Tuesday" changed that. A man named Earl Richardson, an Ontario, California meter reader, began plaguing the power companies to furnish electricity during the day, but only on Tuesday so that women could use the newly invented electric irons. You see Mr. Richardson had another iron in the fire — he had invented a better electric iron, he thought, and he wanted it to be a success. Anyway he was able to prove his point and soon the power companies were generating enough electricity to furnish the homes both day and night — every day. It was needed to operate all the fancy electrical appliances that began flooding the market. Everybody thought they could build a better appliance than anyone else, and many of them did.

The electric steam iron was not introduced until around the mid-1920s. It would be quite a while before it became successful, and several factors contributed to that. One was the price. At that time the average electric iron was selling in the $4 to $6 range while the new steam iron hit the market priced at $10, a much higher price than the women were accustomed to paying. That price was approximately twice as much as the average iron and when compared to salaries at that time, it was just too much. Another problem concerned its usefulness. Would it work and how long would it last? In both cases it has worked well and lasted for years, but the women could not know that when it was first introduced. They did know that a steam iron was not as necessary as the manufacturer might think because at that time the majority of clothes and household linens were starched before hanging on the line. A steam iron was of little use with starched items because as they were dried, each piece was sprinkled (with water), rolled tightly, and wrapped in a heavy cloth, usually a towel. Within a few hours they were ready to be ironed. Pieces that were not ironed that day could be put into the refrigerator and ironed the following day. No longer did they believe everything had to be ironed on Tuesday. But the steam iron that went from one hole in the early days to twenty five or thirty really found its niche in the 1940s with the introduction of synthetic fabrics. The steam iron might not have been useful with starched garments, but it was perfect for the synthetics that needed a controlled heat with just a bit of steam.

During the past century, from 1895 to 1995, we seem to have come full cycle, from ironing everything to ironing nothing. But it has been said that what goes around comes around so we may be on the verge of ironing everything again. It is known that more and more cotton fabrics are being made and less synthetics. We also know that there is lots of interest in irons due to the popularity of all types of old irons. There are a large number of collectors who specialize in old irons, not only sad irons but old electric as well. Generally the collections are mixed to enable the owner to trace the history of irons as well as enjoy all phases of Ironing on Tuesday.

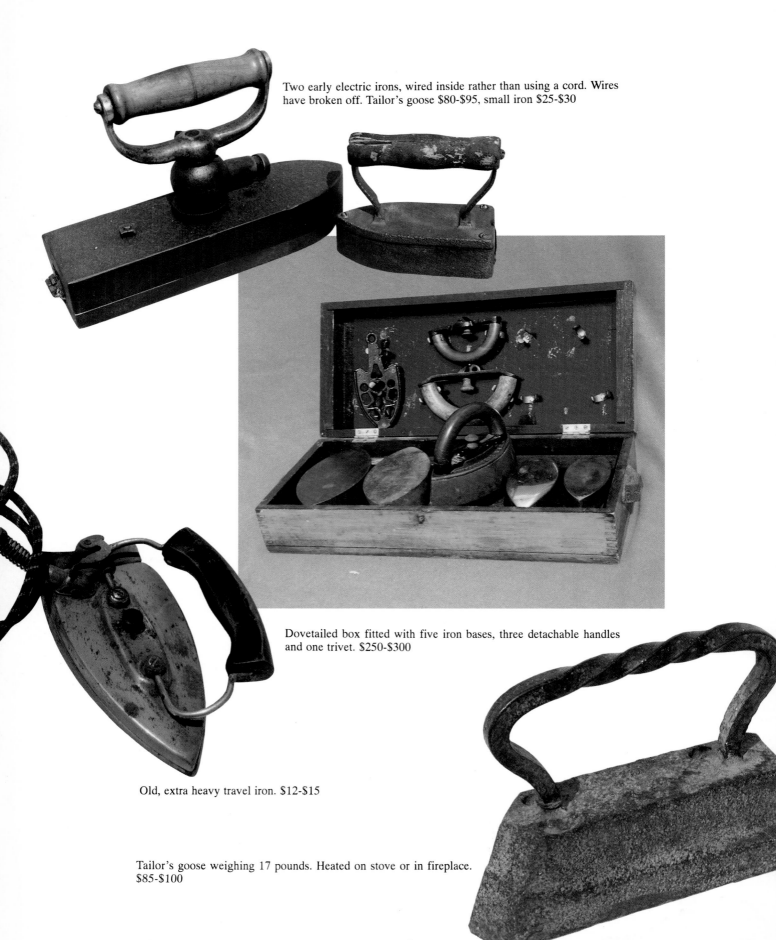

Two early electric irons, wired inside rather than using a cord. Wires have broken off. Tailor's goose $80-$95, small iron $25-$30

Dovetailed box fitted with five iron bases, three detachable handles and one trivet. $250-$300

Old, extra heavy travel iron. $12-$15

Tailor's goose weighing 17 pounds. Heated on stove or in fireplace. $85-$100

Iron with an unusual plug, required a special cord. $20-$25

Same iron as above, but with cord plugged in.

These irons usually came with three or four bases and one lift-off handle that could be transferred from one hot iron to another. $35-$45

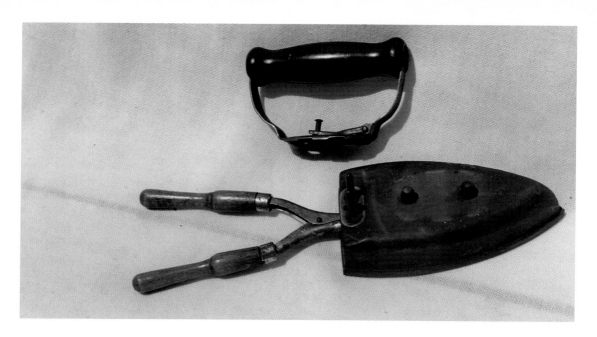

Electric iron that has space for heating hair curlers. Handle can be removed. $35-$40

Presto electric iron with original box and trivet. Circa 1950. $19-$30

Two sad irons. $16-$22 each

Different style sad iron. $15-$19

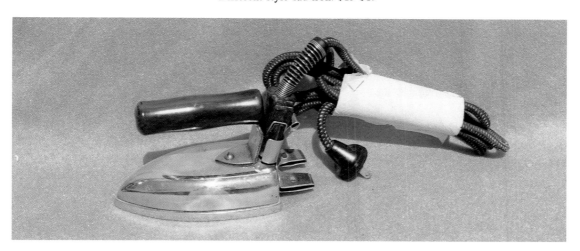

Electric iron with open handle. $16-$22

Three trivets, could be used for sad irons or electric examples. Were used to keep the hot iron off the ironing board where the hot iron would either burn or scorch the cover. $9-$12 each

113

Two of these trivets are three deckers while one is wide spaced to protect the ironing board cover. $10-$13 each

Blue enameled Coleman iron that used white gasoline. Circa 1920. $50-$75

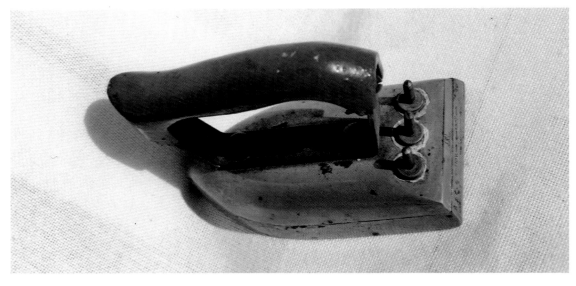

Unusual electric iron in that it has three prongs requiring a different type cord. $25-$30

114

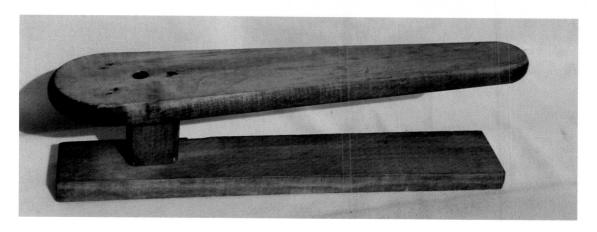

Sleeve ironing board, uncovered. $12-$14

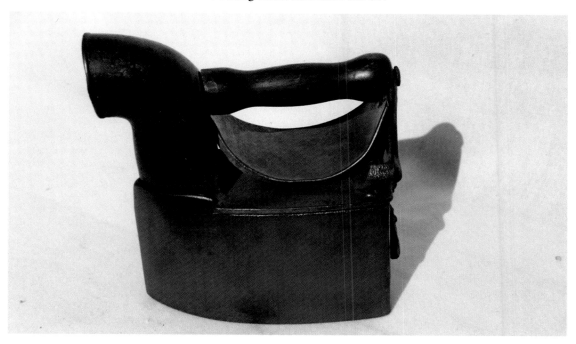

So-called box iron that could be heated either with a lug or charcoal.
$35-$40

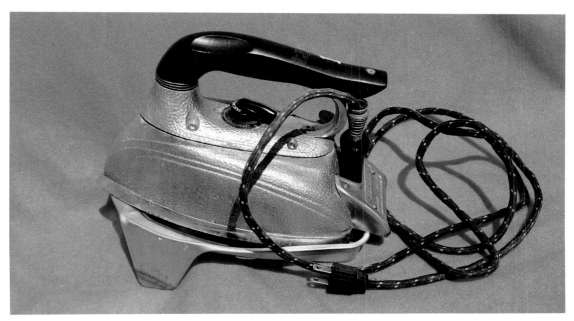

Aluminum, Steam-O-Matic electric iron and trivet. $35-$45

Brass Chinese iron was filled with charcoal for ironing. $20-$25

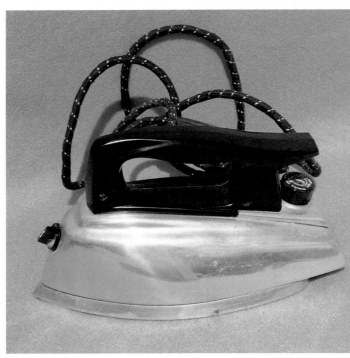

Electric steam iron with water filler cap on the front of the iron. $20-$25

Electric iron with thumb rest. $15-$20

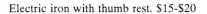

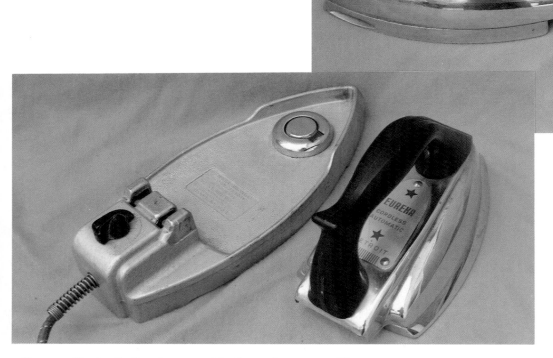

The name Eureka Cordless Iron was a bit of an understatement. The iron was cordless while the base or trivet had a cord. The iron was placed on the trivet for heating. $35-$50

Chapter Twelve
Learning Tools for Girls

Almost from the beginning of time until World War II girls did not expect to have jobs, good jobs that they would keep until they retired. Up until the early Forties the best most of them could hope for was a job that paid a small salary so they could buy pretty clothes. The idea here was to look as beautiful as possible because they believed that beautiful, well dressed girls had a better chance of attracting wealthy men. In fact, the advice given most girls was "It is as easy to love a rich man as a poor one." But that all changed with the war. The men went off to fight while the girls took the good paying jobs, mostly defense jobs. Finally, they could support themselves, they were not dependent on a husband, and they would never be satisfied to stay home and do housework full time again. Prior to that time girls were trained to become housewives and only housewives, but before that happened they had to get married. The second part of the last sentence tells the whole story – from birth the girls were trained in housekeeping duties. The theory being that girls who excelled in home making had less trouble getting a husband. Since the only alternative was spinsterhood, they strived to learn all the chores necessary to make the home attractive.

When they were older they would help their mothers with the real household chores, but as young children they had play houses complete with dolls that represented children and a complete layout of small furniture and cooking tools and utensils. This way they learned everything they needed to know – one step at a time. Big families were absolutely essential, therefore they also had to learn to be good mothers, hence the dolls. Additionally they were taught to take care of their toys which

accounts for so many being available today. Surprisingly, it is the adults who are today so avidly collecting those miniature toys of a half century or so ago. After analyzing that statement perhaps those collectors today are the same children who played with the toys earlier. Most collectors are trying to recreate memories of the happier times of their childhood.

In an effort to make the girls entirely responsible for every phase of homemaking, they were also taught basket making, especially in families where the craft was important. They usually learned by making what was known as penny baskets, a simple little basket that sold for a penny. As they grew more skilled they made other types including many miniatures. The latter was important teaching tools as they could understand and were eager to make baskets that were small and would fit nicely into their playhouses. It all depended on where they grew up as to which type they made. In the areas where splint baskets were more popular, they would more than likely make that kind. Indian children were taught basket making at an early age, and they also made baskets like those made by their mothers. In the south it would be river or swamp cane while in the northeast they preferred sweet grass and ash splints.

Many fathers, especially the ones who were skilled whittlers, made toys for their children. In fact, one father made the little black stove patterned after the old woodburning stove the mother used. It has dovetailed corners, eyes that are just indented in the wood, and a door that opens to expose the oven. Then there were factory made toys like the tiny brass mortars and pestles, the small, tin cake pans, and the small muffin pans. One middle aged woman remembers well when her mother prepared for a child's birthday party by baking a couple dozen small, decorated muffins or cup cakes. Her theory was a child might not want a large muffin and would waste at least half of it. If they wanted more than the small muffin, they could have more without wasting food. People at that time were still in the throes of the former waste not-want not generation.

Among the small wooden tools made for the girls were potato mashers and rolling pins. They are most attractive when displayed on a board, possibly under a narrow shelf in the kitchen. For a real primitive look they can be displayed on one half of a mule's hame. Or they can be displayed on a board like the small graniteware cooking tools and utensils. This set, the only complete one we have ever seen was found in Kentucky about 25 years ago and bought by a collector in Ohio. Because it was so complete and so outstanding, the collector paid the $500 price without a murmur.

Other pieces made especially for the girls are the little sad irons with their special trivets. The iron with the lift-off top is older than the one with the painted design which dates around the early Fifties. The iron replica of the large, store model of the coffee mill is about the same age as it was found advertised in a 1950s catalog from a Pennsylvania store of the Amish. The date the little coffee mill on the wooden base was made is unknown, but chances are it is about the same age as the large, store model mill.

Small egg beaters and whisks were also made for the little girls, but the ones found now seem to date around the Fifties and Sixties, maybe later. Whether they were made much earlier is unknown. But it is known that miniature iron pots and pans have been made for a century or more. The old iron bean pot was so necessary and so well known, it is small wonder so many of them were made. They are not as easy to find today as they were even a decade ago. Apparently they have disappeared into private collections or maybe into museums as many of them are showing later things these days.

Set of thirteen small playhouse pieces of graniteware cooking utensils for little girls. Was often sold with a small replica of the old wood burning cookstove. Twenty years ago this set sold for $500. Rare. Today's price $2,000 to $3,000.

Small cast aluminum bowl and pitcher. $25-30

Then there are the small things that defy the identification of their original use, that is, were they originally made as salesmen's samples or as children's toys. A case in point is the adorable copper chafing dish. Approximately 5.5 inches to the top of the finial and nearly 4 inches in diameter it could pass for either. But the one thing that seems to qualify it as a salesman's sample is the quality of the workmanship and the materials. It is so well made that had it been a toy it would have probably cost more than most families could afford. Both workmanship and materials are of the best quality, and it has never been used although the lamp is ready for use. The water pan is made of heavy copper while the food pan is tinned inside. This seems to have been extra work and expense for a child's toy that would never have been used to prepare food anyway. On the other hand the company probably would have tinned the inside to show the merchant how well the larger chafing dishes were made. Like the large chafing dishes the legs are brass. For years all collectors have argued about the difference between toys and salesman's sample. Unless we can find proof that they were originally one or the other, the discussions will probably go on. In the meantime collectors will continue to categorize all of these small pieces according to their own ideas.

Two playhouse sized loaf pans. Larger one 3.5 by 5.75 inches. Marked Ecko. $5-$6. Smaller one 2.75 by 4.5 inches. unmarked. $6-$9

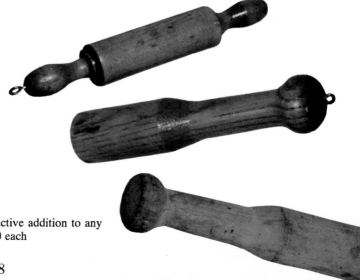

Small rolling pin and two grinders. Makes attractive addition to any kitchen when hung under open shelves. $15-$20 each

118

Small handmade replica of the old wood burning cookstove. Appears to have been made from an old wooden packing box. Probably made for some child's playhouse. $200-$500

Small Choctaw-made, river cane basket, 1.5 inches in diameter, 3 inches to top of handle. $100-$150

Small iron, store-type coffee grinder. 4 inches tall, 2.5 inches across the widest part. Would have been wonderful for kids who also had a general store in their play area. $45-$60

Small coffee mill, accurate in every detail, drawer missing. 2.5 inches square, 3.5 inches to top of handle. $35-$40

Iron posnet, 2 inches tall, 5 inches to end of handle. $50-$75

Miniature copper chafing dish believed to be a salesman's sample, but could have been made for children. 4 inches in diameter, 5 inches tall. $65-$75

Small copper chafing dish showing inside.

Small copper skillet with brass lid. Tinned, 4.5 inches in diameter. $10-$15

Making these small baskets was training for young girls. The parents thought there would always be a demand for baskets. They sold for one to five cents half a century ago. This one is 2.25 inches in diameter, 3 inches to top of handle. $25-$30

Small buttocks basket made of finely cut white oak splints about the size of coarse thread, 3 inches in diameter, 4 inches to top of handle. Due to expert workmanship, will sell for about $200 to $250 today.

Small basket, 3 inches long, 2.5 inches wide, 2 inches to top of handle. $25-$35

Brass candle holder for seven candles. It is 3.5 inches across, 2.5 inches tall. $30-$40

Tiny brass mortar and pestle. Mortar 1 inch tall, same in diameter, pestle 1.5 inches long. $12-$15

Late child's size sad iron and trivet, decorated. Circa 1955. $35-$40

Two small irons and trivets, left is old with detachable handle, $40-45, right painted set $35-$40.

Small aluminum skillet, 5 inches in diameter. $10-$12

Aluminum plate, cup, and saucer from a child's tea set. $23-$27

Chapter Thirteen
Miscellaneous

Miscellaneous is a magnificent word for pulling together all the loose ends of any endeavor, especially books. There are always those one-of-a-kind left-overs that refuse to fit into any of the existing categories, yet there are not enough of each to build a new category. A case in point is the cane bottomed chair. Since this book was organized to show the small things one could use to give an antique look to a modern kitchen, a furniture category was not planned. But this chair and others like it have such a marvelous history, we felt it should be included. They all started out the same, that is the seat on all of them started out the same height from the floor, but as the covered wagons rumbled southward and westward they found that shorter legs made the chairs more steady, they didn't turn over as easily when the ruts were deep and rough. It might even be a small wagon train, maybe only three or four wagons, but as soon as they discovered the convenience of the lower chairs, the legs were sawed off to make a chair's legs about twelve to thirteen inches tall. Not being a wasteful people they did not throw away the chairs when they arrived at their new homes. Instead they used them while performing the daily chore of churning the milk to make butter. They were a perfect height, so eventually they became known as "churn chairs."

Another odd piece is the old water dipper made from a gourd. When they were first made the family searched for the gourd with the straightest handle so it could be hung by the well easily. Since there are no longer any wells and few springs, the gourd dipper has become an "artsy" item that people decorate with designs and sell to the tourists. The shape of the handle is of little interest, probably because the crooked handle fits in better with the painted design. A leather throng is put through a hole in the handle for hanging. Another gourd item that fits into the kitchen decor is one from Africa that, according to the original owner, started life as a salt gourd but by his own admission could be used for any chore that fits.

Cocktail shakers are not as much kitchen oriented as they are bar. Nevertheless the gleaming silver brightens up any kitchen decor. Scales were once an important part of any kitchen.

They were needed for weighing anything produced on the farm and sold — from butter to honey. Many collectors only collect scales, all the different kinds from those with brass fronts to steelyards. Ordinary examples are easily found, but the unusual are both scarce and expensive.

Stoneware is one of the antiques that is avidly sought by collectors. Some collectors concentrate on it and have fabulous collections of the finest and rarest pieces while others only want a few items to use as accent pieces. In the northeast bean pots are extremely popular, probably because baked beans were one of the staple foods for a century or so. Older men still remember one of their weekly chores when boys. Their mothers filled the bean pot with her seasoned beans and the young boys took them to the bakery or communal oven depending on the area — always on Saturday. In some areas they were baked at home, again it depended on the area. The beans were ready by evening when the boy returned to pick up the pot. The family ate baked beans for supper that night and, what may sound unusual to some of us, they had a cold bean sandwich for breakfast on Sunday morning. Baked beans are still an important food in the northeast, but people seldom bake their own anymore. But the memory of them lingers, and they want the bean pots for nostalgia. Through the years so many lids were broken that collectors have to search now to find a complete one, but those without lids make excellent holders for knives and other cooking tools. In fact, most of the smaller stoneware pieces are not only decorative, but useful as containers in the kitchen.

In the 1940s if the women wanted to be daring, they crocheted pot holders in the shape of women's underwear. In those days the pot holders were considered rather naughty, after all this was a time when no sex and very little kissing was shown on the screen. Instead the couple kissed a couple of times and the scene faded into the sunset. Women's undies were described as unmentionables and they were never shown except in catalogues like Sears — and in the kitchen of the most daring. The pot holders were made by the dozens and given to friends and neighbors. Some were used; others packed away which explains why so many perfect examples can still be found today. Surprisingly, they seem to be rather popular as they sell well at flea markets and some antique malls. When asked, the buyers say they want to create a kitchen like their mother or grandmother had — depending, of course, on their age.

Unusual jar and can openers have always intrigued collectors. The can opener with the wooden handle has no information, but is believed to have been a new invention, probably patented. Since we have been unable to figure out how it works, it might not have been popular enough to have become a best seller, which explains why this version is so scarce. The jar opener is a little easier to use as it is logical that if the notch on the handle is pressed against the ridges of the lid, it will naturally loosen it. Women who canned their own fruit and vegetables have always been partial to glass jars, most with metal lids. They had to be tightened very tight to keep the fruit and vegetables from spoiling, and when they were that tight, it was not easy getting them open later when the contents were needed.

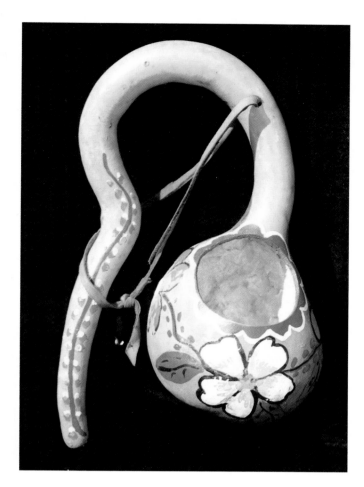

Decorated gourd dipper, sold to tourists. $10-$12

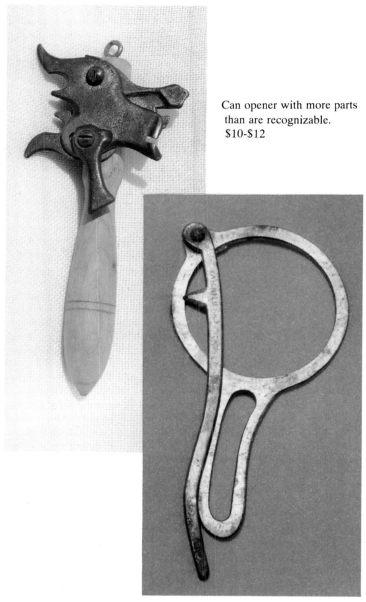

Can opener with more parts than are recognizable. $10-$12

In areas where maple trees are plentiful, the owners usually save the sap when it is running to make syrup or candy. At one time nearly every family made their own syrup and candy, but in recent years it has become more commercialized. The relics of this earlier maple candy making that are most sought after are the molds. All types and designs were made from the shallow to the deep. Designs varied from very plain to very ornate. Like everything else, it depended on the whims and the skills of the maker. Today these older molds are quite scarce and rather expensive when found.

Centuries ago the Indian bowl was the kitchen, the only thing they had that resembled a place to cook and eat their food. The food was usually cooked in the bowls they made — over a fire outside the house or tepee. The meal could be served in smaller bowls or it could be eaten from the one in which it was cooked. So, there is no way we can not associate those bowls with kitchens.

Today Indian-made bowls are so scarce and so expensive no one uses them for cooking anymore — or for serving; however, Indian bowls are used to decorate modern kitchens as well as dining rooms, keeping rooms, dens, and even living rooms. But their origin is still in the kitchen.

Fruit jars that had been sealed were hard to open, openers were almost essential. $10-$12

Small hanging scales made by Chatillon, New York. $18-$20

125

This is one of the chairs that was cut down so it would not topple over when riding in the wagon. $50-$100

Green Depression glass salt and pepper shakers, aluminum tops. $18-$24

African-made gourd salt box. $20-$25

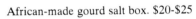

Southwest Indian bowl marked E. Garcia, Acoma, N.M. $500-$800

126

Silver-plated cocktail shaker. $24-$30

Two small stoneware crocks excellent now for holding and displaying small kitchen tools. $25-$50 each

Naughty, crocheted undies made for pot holders in the 1930s and '40s. $2-$4 each

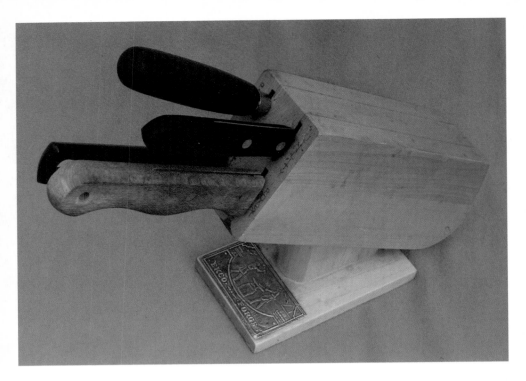

Wooden knife rack, marked Ekco Forge. Rack only $15-$22

Late brown and white bean pot, missing lid. $20-$25

Wooden maple candy mold. $35-$50

Chapter Fourteen
Mixers, Food and Beverage

In their 1929-30 catalogue Wetmore-Savage Electrical Supply Company, a Westinghouse Agent-Jobber with branches in Boston, Worchester, and Springfield, Massachusetts, Providence, Rhode, Island, and Bangor, Maine only showed one food mixer. It was described as a Dormeyer beater and mixer. Actually it was about the same as the electric hand mixers today with a motor on one side of the top and a handle beside it. It was described as a time and labor saver for the modern kitchen, and was further described as "A fast, thorough beating, 8-blade, double-acting beater of improved Dover design." According to the description it had a 110-volt Hamilton Beach universal motor, variable speeds (not specified), and a right and left-hand rheostat switch. A 6-foot cord and plug completed the description except for the weight which was 3.5 pounds. There was no stand. There were also neither bowls nor accessories as the later mixer had, yet the price was $22.50 — and in the latter part of 1929 and early 1930. Apparently, the catalogue was printed before the Wall Street crash, but that price seems a bit high even for the so-called boom year of 1929.

They showed a couple of Hamilton Beach drink mixers, the model with the chrome cup being almost identical to one used in the illustrations. That mixer came with the upright in four different colors, jade green, ivory, jet black, and snow white. The white was priced at $22 while the ones in color were $23.50 each. The drink mixer operated, they said, on 105-120 volts, a.c. or d.c., 26-60 cycles. It came with a chromium-plated cup and a six foot cord and plug (no mention is made of a cord and plug on electrical appliances today because they are standard equipment). It was packed in a wooden box with a total weight of 16 pounds.

Everything moved more slowly in those days, but by 1941 a tremendous amount of progress had been made, especially in food mixers. According to full page descriptions of several mixers in Carson Pirie Scott and Company's wholesale catalogue that year, the mixers were as advanced as they are today, maybe more so as they had so many attachments, especially the Sunbeam Mixmaster. A page was required just to show the mixer and explain the "new, exclusive automatic mix-finder" which was a dial on the back that found the correct speed for any mixing chore. One of the things that was especially interesting and completely in tune with the times was the statement that it had a non-radio interfering motor. Remember this was a time when the phonograph was losing its popularity and radio was the main form of entertainment. Television was not yet available, but then as now any interference with the entertainment caused trouble in the family. Another interesting notation was it had a salad-oil dropper that facilitated making mayonnaise. So few people make their own mayonnaise today that this feature certainly would not be a big selling point. The mixer came in two colors with bowls that matched each. Two jade green bowls came with the one in ivory finish while white bowls came with the black and white one. Without the juice extractor the retail price was $21; with the extractor it cost $23.75.

Over a dozen extra attachments were offered including an extra power unit that was required to operate the food chopper, meat grinder, coffee grinder, colander for ricing potatoes or for purees of all kinds, sieving or creaming bananas, and for using the can opener. The price of this power unit was $2.75 retail. All prices given on the mixers and attachments were retail. The bean slicer was $2, coffee grinder $2.50, knife sharpener $3.50, ice cream freezer unit that would turn the freezer until the ice cream was made $3.50, potato peeler $5, pea sheller $2, can opener $2, slicer and shredder $6.50, colander $4.50, food chopper-meat grinder $6.50, and the butter churn attachment that looks much like the Dazey churn that is so collectible today was $3.95. A polisher-buffer that was described as perfect for keeping the silverware and all metal finishes bright and shining could be bought for 75 cents. A drink mixer could be bought for $2.50 and attached to the mixer. This eliminated the need for an extra beverage mixer; in fact, so many of these attachments eliminated the needs for old tools and utensils, it is small wonder they were discarded in favor of the new easy-to-use electric ones. That in turn would explain the loss of so many of the old handmade kitchen tools and utensils.

When the new mixers with all their attachments began appearing on the market, many homemakers wanted the new labor saving devices, but were not sure they would do the job. To be on the safe side they stored the old handmade things in the basement or attic just in case those new-fangled contraptions didn't work. They did work and the stored things were forgotten for years. In many cases when they found they were antiques and collectibles and tried to retrieve them, they had deteriorated.

In the same catalogue there was a full page advertisement for the new Universal food mixer and about a half page on the Hamilton Beach. The Universal stressed the fact that an extra power unit was not necessary. They did not advertise as many attachments as the Sunbeam and several, like the pea huller and bean slicer, were combination attachments. The cost of $3.75 for this attachment was comparable to the Sunbeam's two pieces. Hamilton Beach offered the same combination attachment for $2.45 proving you had to shop as carefully then as now.

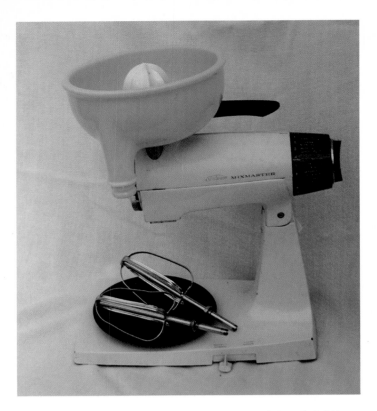

Sunbeam Mixmaster electric food mixer with green juicer. $18-$33

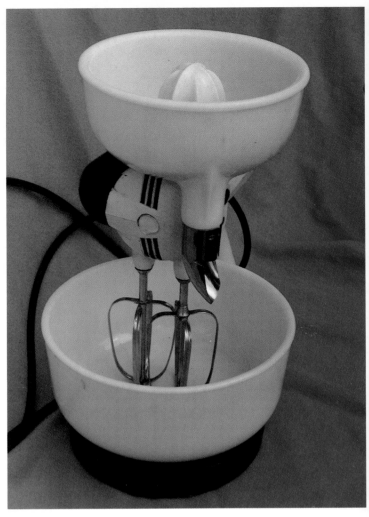

With the price of new electric food mixers hovering around $90 now, it has been noticeable lately how many young women are buying the old mixers either at yard sales, flea markets, or antique malls. The prices there have increased unbelievably during the past few years. Half a dozen years ago food mixers could be found at most yard sales priced around $3 to $5 each. Some came with attachments, others didn't. Last week a mixer that was about the same as those seen previously was priced $25 at a yard sale. When they were selling in the $3 to $5 range at yard sales they were easily found at antique malls and flea markets priced around $15. Recently one was seen there priced $65. The only conclusion one can arrive at is that the old ones are getting more collectible, or they are being bought instead of new ones.

In fact, it has recently become quite obvious that all old electrical appliances are becoming quite popular, now whether as collectibles or to be used is unknown. But we can not stress the fact to much that some of these appliances may not be safe to use as found. Electric cords and plugs are the danger points. Be sure to check them carefully before using, and if there seems to be the slightest danger, either fix them yourself or take them to a hardware store that repairs appliances. There may even be a man in your area who specializes in repairing electrical appliances.

On the older appliances it would probably be safer to have complete new wiring before using it.

Electric mixer with juicer on top. With bowl and juicer $25-$40

New electric mixers are high priced today which makes the older ones more valuable. Close-up of juicer.

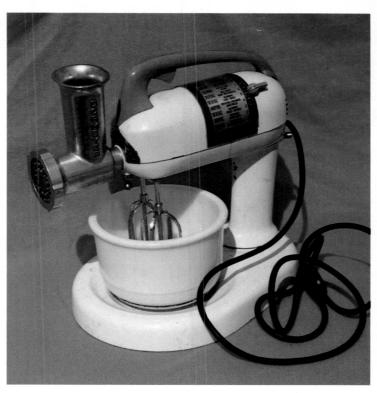

Dormeyer food mixer with food chopper, many of the small tools that came with the mixers in the 1940s and '50s. $29-$39

Sunbeam electric mixer, circa 1950. $20-$30

Electric Kitchen Aid food mixer. $27-$33

Old electric Hamilton Beach food mixer. $32-$38

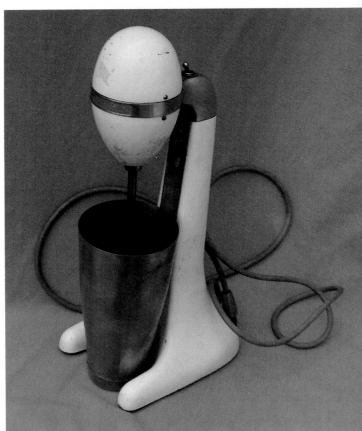

Twenty five years ago women with any artistic talent decorated old, discarded kitchen utensils, not only to decorate their own kitchens, but to sell. This mixer seems to be a left over from the 1950-60 decorating craze. $15-$35

Hamilton Beach beverage mixer. $22-$28

Gilbert beverage mixer. $25-$32

Old General Electric food mixer, probably more valuable as a collectible than for use although it still works. $32-$39

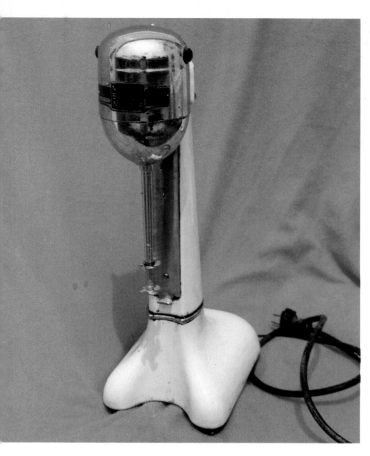

Myers Bullet beverage mixer. $19-$30

General Electric food mixer with three beaters. $35-$42

An older General Electric food mixer. $28-$35

Hamilton Beach electric food mixer with juicer. $30-$40

Late Hamilton Beach beverage mixer. $24-$30

Westinghouse electric food mixer, juicer has metal strainer. $32-$38

Hamilton Beach electric food mixer. $24-$27

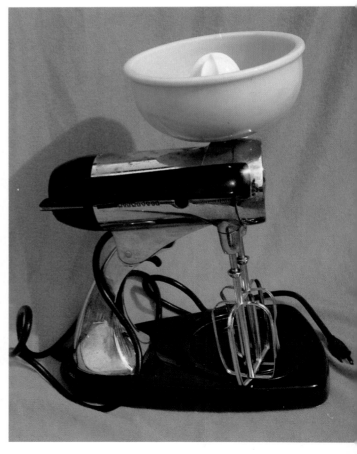

Partially chrome electric food mixer has handle that turns over so juicer will fit. $38-$45

Chapter Fifteen
Roasters, Toasters, Peels, Molds, and Poppers

The role of the homemaker has changed drastically during the past century, but if we go back to the early days, those days when the early settlers were trying to get their houses in order, we can really see the changes. Even though things seemed to move slowly in those early days, nevertheless there were tremendous changes all brought about by the invention of more and better labor saving devices. Whereas some of those early settlers had to survive on corn dishes, pumpkins, various berries, fish, and game, the work was not so much in preparing it as finding and gathering it. Even when they acquired cattle, chickens, and sheep, more labor was required just to feed them and milk the cows. It seemed there was no end to their labors so it is easy to see why they gladly accepted any new labor saving device that came their way.

Homemakers were delighted when ovens were built into the sides of the fireplaces so they could bake without the use of the Dutch oven that had to have hot coals heaped on top of it. Then when the peel was invented, they were probably overcome with joy. The peel was a long handled gadget with a wide flat surface on one end. It could be made of iron at the blacksmith shop or made of wood. Either way it allowed the cook to remove bread or cakes from the oven without burning her hands or her face. The peel was abandoned when the woodburning stove became a reality.

Although there was still lots of work for the homemaker in the Twenties and Thirties, it was much easier than it had been previously. So many labor saving devices had been invented and by that time people in the larger cities and towns were getting electricity. Add that to the many appliances that were being made regularly, and you had a bunch of happy homemakers. Prior to that time, food was prepared in the kitchen and served at the table in the dining room. With the invention of the electric toaster that all changed. Breakfast might still be prepared in the kitchen, but toast as well as waffles and coffee were made at the table using the new electrical makers. From looking at old advertisements it seems Sunbeam was a leader in the field of daring new introductions. By 1940 they were offering a new automatic toaster buffet set that consisted of the toaster itself along with four lap trays (no explanation was given for their use unless they were to replace breakfast plates), and a three compartment appetizer dish of Intaglio Crystal, all on a large, roomy walnut tray. The retail price of this set was $23.

The word mold covers a multitude of items when it is used in connection with the kitchen or cooking because so many dishes required a mold of some kind. Molds have been used for bread, puddings, candy, ice cream, cheese, butter, cakes, cookies, and maple sugar candy. Other molds have been covered in this book, but here it is mostly cakes, puddings, and jellies — particularly Calf's Feet jelly that was so popular from the late 1600s through the 1800s. Through the years, various kinds of molds have been made using practically every known material from pewter to aluminum. Of course the early molds were made of pewter as it was the most popular material for all types of kitchen tools and utensils. Old pewter ice cream molds can still be found. Iron was popular for some molds including the one used to make hog's head cheese or souse. A heavy pottery that would almost pass for stoneware, or maybe it was a fine grade of stoneware, was made in the 1800s. These molds had very ornate designs in the bottom, everything from an ear of corn to grapes.

Of course in later years the molds were used more often for Jello and salads, but in those early days the favorite was jelly, especially Calf's Feet Jelly. Maybe the younger collector will appreciate the molds more when they learn how they were first used. To accomplish that a recipe from an 1865 English cook book follows. The description and word usage may be a bit strange at times, but remember it is about 130 years old. The author began with:

"We hear inexperienced housekeepers frequently complain of the difficulty of rendering this jelly transparent; but by mixing with the other ingredients, while quite cold, the whites and the crushed shells of a sufficient number of eggs, and allowing the head of scum which gathers on the jelly to remain undisturbed after it once forms, they will scarcely fail to obtain it clear. It should be strained through a thick flannel, or beaver-skin bag of a conical form."

It was suggested that if the jelly was not perfectly clear after straining, it would have to be strained over and over until it was. To obtain the broth from which the jelly would be made, she suggested fresh calf's feet should be bought from the butcher (remember this was 1865), the feet scalded to remove the hair and hooves. After much washing the feet were boiled until the meat left the bones. This formed the broth needed to make the jelly. But back to the original recipe:

"Mix thoroughly in a large stew pan five half-pints of strong calf's feet stock, a full pint of sherry, half a pound of sugar roughly powdered, the juice of two fine lemons, the rind of one and a half cut very thin, the whites and shells of four large eggs, and half an ounce of isinglass."

Knapp-Monarch electric Redi-Oven for roasting or baking. $15-$20

This mixture was allowed to remain off the fire for a few minutes so the sugar would dissolve more. Then it was brought to a boil slowly, but was not stirred at all during that time. "When it has boiled gently for 16 minutes," she wrote, "draw it from the fire, and let it stand for a short time before it is poured into a jelly bag, under which a bowl should be placed to receive it. When clear and cool, put it into molds which have been laid for some hours in water; these should always be of earthenware in preference to metal."

For some this dish would not only be difficult to make today while for others it lacks something in the appetizing department. It would appear that expense was the most important factor in making this jelly at that time, and there are indications that homemakers preferred one with less alcoholic contents, especially for the young people as the author suggested using good orange or raisin wine instead of sherry for them. And she went on to explain that "excellent jellies are made with calves' feet, variously flavored." For adults she suggested using a fine liqueur as a substitute for the sherry. It was also suggested that fresh strawberries could be dropped into the jelly before it set to add to the appearance as well as the taste. Perhaps the most interesting statement in the several pages of calves' feet jelly recipes was the advice that along with the liqueur the hostess might want to add vanilla, cinnamon or Seville orange rind. "For the aristocratic table," she wrote, "indeed, it is the present fashion to serve them (jellies) very lightly and delicately flavored."

Since the Pilgrims arrived, corn has played an important role in our lives. In the beginning it was used in everything from ground meal carried dry by the hunter and eaten that way to hasty pudding, mush, corn meal pudding, Indian pudding, samp, or bannock cakes. The people moving westward and southward learned a new method for cooking the corn meal mixed with water. They put it on the iron head of a hoe, then propped it in front of the fire where it cooked. They called them "hoe cakes." When this same mixture is cooked on a griddle on the stove it becomes a "corn pone."

All of the corn had to be cooked or baked before it could be ground for any of the dishes, and somewhere in that era of inventiveness somebody discovered certain types of corn would pop, hence the name popcorn. With all kinds of toppings, popcorn soon became a delicacy, and then a snack food. Through the years, everybody had their favorite popcorn popper. It might be a wire or mesh model or tin with large holes, but they all had a long handle so they could be held over the fire or the stove. Then electricity arrived on the scene and the variety of electrical popcorn poppers that became available was mind boggling. Today the older ones are being collected to be used as they always have been while some are bought to display with collections of older electrical appliances. Be sure to check the wiring on all appliances and especially popcorn poppers before using them.

During the Industrial Revolution when everybody was trying to build a better mouse trap than anyone else, a few people tried their hand at inventing roasters, and a few succeeded. The improvement was in developing roasting pans to replace the open tin roasters the early settlers had used to roast birds in front of their open fires. With ovens and stoves it was no longer necessary to use them; a covered roasting pan was sufficient. But the big breakthrough came just before World War II with the invention of the Automatic Electric Roaster. It was a 24 inch long, 18 inch wide, and 13 inch tall covered roaster that came with a cooking well that would hold several dishes to be cooked at once. It had a dial that allowed the heat to be controlled exactly, and it was hailed as one of the greatest inventions for the busy housewife, therefore it was no surprise when the majority of new housewives, those married to returning servicemen, bought one. The price was $35 for the average type. Like all the other modern inventions of that era they have been replaced with even more modern inventions like the microwave oven. But every now and then one of those old ovens will be seen in a yard sale or an estate sale, and it is nice to add one to any growing collection of early electrical appliances.

Early electric, four-slice toaster made by The Nelson Machine and Manufacturing Company, Cleveland, Ohio. $18-$26

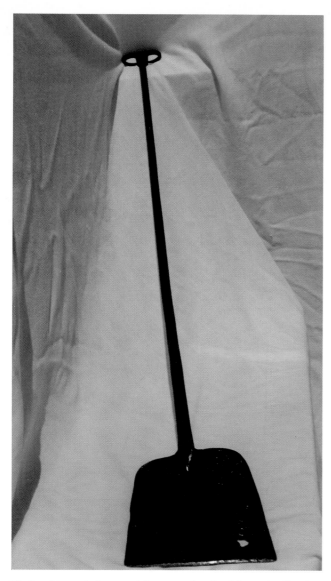

Blacksmith-made iron peel for removing food from the fireplace ovens. $75-$100

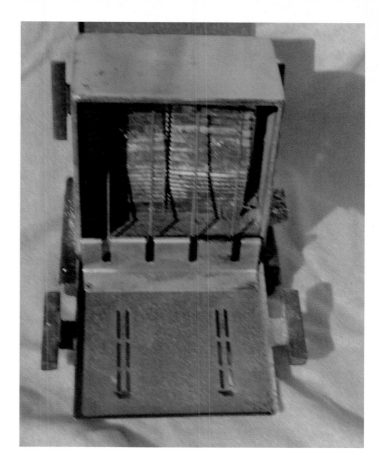

Empire toaster open to show inside.

Empire two-slice toaster made by The Metal Ware Corporation, Two Rivers, Wisconsin. $20-$30

Manning Bowman early electric toaster. $30-$35

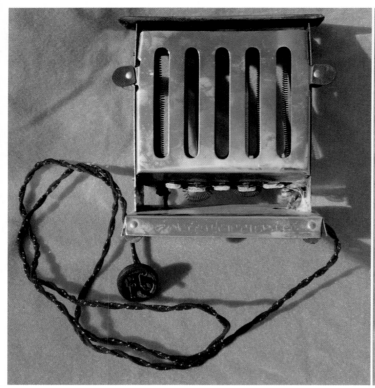

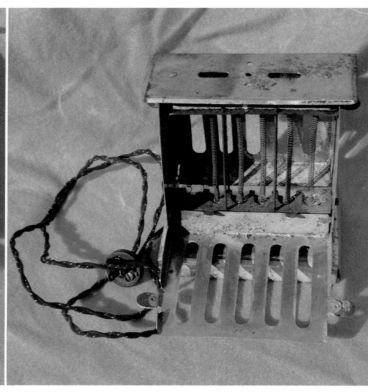

Early electric two-slice toaster made by Capitol Products, Winsted, Connecticut. $28-$35

Capitol Products toaster, opened to show how the bread slid down on the door for turning — to toast on the other side.

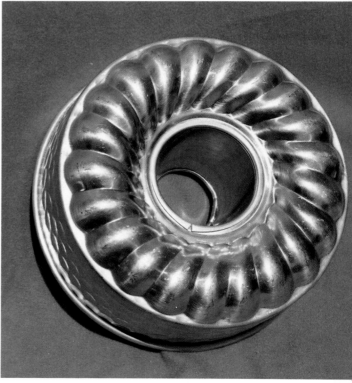

Sunbeam electric toaster with wide, vertical holes for the bread. Circa 1940. $15-$19

Large, round aluminum mold. $12-15

Copper mold, fruit design in bottom. $15-$18

Plain tin mold with fluted sides. $10-$12

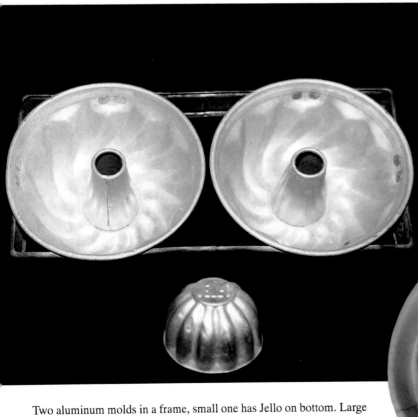

Two aluminum molds in a frame, small one has Jello on bottom. Large $20/23, Jello $7-$8

Old pottery mold with ear of corn design in bottom. $75-$100

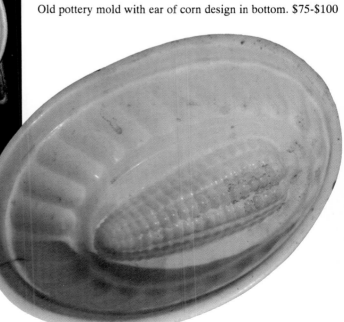

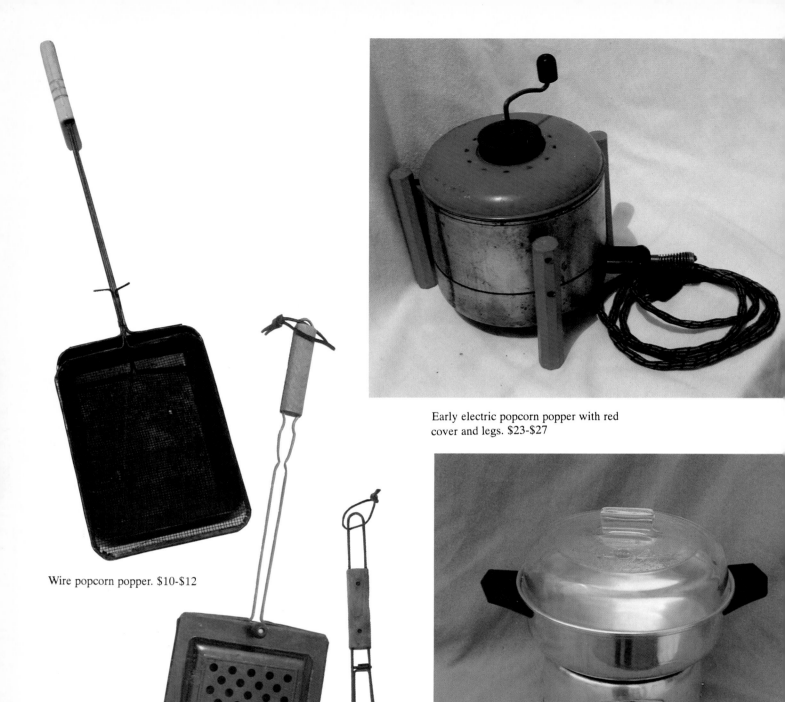

Wire popcorn popper. $10-$12

Early electric popcorn popper with red
cover and legs. $23-$27

Black tin over-the-fire popcorn popper. $9-$12

Knapp-Monarch electric Redi-Pop popcorn popper. $15-$20

Mesh, over-the-fire popcorn popper. $9-$12

Chapter Sixteen
Sieves, Sifters, Trays, Trivets, and Rolling Pins

Sieves (that have also been known by names like sifters, riddles, and bolters (a very old name)) are among those kitchen utensils that saw a lot of use in the past. In fact, as late as half a century ago it would have been hard to find a country home without at least three or four different kinds of sifters. First, there was the one that was always kept in the flour barrel because even then farm folk traded some of their corn meal for flour. Since it was ground at the same mill — always a water mill — as the corn, both needed sifting to remove the fine husks that remained. Most families in those days had two barrels, one for freshly ground cornmeal and the other for flour, in the pantry, and each had its own sifter. At this late date most of the sifters were factory-made, usually of tin with screen wire in the bottom to catch the husks. But in earlier days they had usually been handmade and could be made of basketry, woodenware with horsehair in the bottom, or old tin. One wooden sifter used in the illustrations has a bottom made of rather widely-spaced, narrow splints. Then there is the very unusual one that appears to have been made out of coiled rye and covered with sheep skin. The holes in the bottom are very even and so small one wonders about its original use. But as we have said so many times our ancestors were an ingenious lot, and if a strange chore came up, one they had not had before and probably would not encounter again, they simply made a tool to fit it.

Corn furnished more than just cornbread. Grits and hominy were, and still are, made from corn. Grits are a coarsely ground corn, coarser than cornmeal, and usually made at home until the last half century or so. Hominy is made from the whole kernel.

In the beginning, the Indians cooked it in hot ashes, and when the Pilgrims arrived they taught them that method. Much later the settlers learned how to obtain the same results by boiling the corn in water with just a bit of lye added. No matter which method was used the husk or hull separated from the kernels. To remove the husks another type of sieve was necessary.

Southern Indians made a lovely hominy sieve using river or swamp cane. It is not that different from other shallow baskets except it has wide weaving in the bottom to allow the husks to escape. Some of the makers dyed strips of cane so they could make a design in the sieve. Hominy sieves were made in other areas as well, but our research shows that different materials were used in each. For example, in the northeast poplar and ash splints were used.

Another type of sieve that is still made today by the southern Indians is the combination sieve and basket. They are made now to sell to the tourists more than to use. They are made of river or swamp cane with the smaller, open-weave sieve used for sifting and the solid-weave bottom basket used to catch the meal as it is sifted through. The husks stays in the top.

The most interesting and the most sought after of all sieves is the one made with a horsehair bottom. Controversy surrounds this one as some say human hair rather than horse hair was used to make it. Then there are those who think possibly any hair from that of a human to that from a horse's mane or tail was used. Some even say the hair from a cow's tail was used. Regardless of what was used, they are always referred to simply as horsehair sieves. Due to the fine texture of the hair some of them are a bit delicate looking, and the design on some looks like Tartan plaids, especially when dark and light hair is used in combination. The finest of the horsehair sieves have been credited to the Shakers, and it is believed they made the first ones of this type. It is also a known fact that the neighbors of the Shakers, both Indians and whites, especially in Maine, copied things made by the Shakers to sell to the tourists. The Shakers were always well known for their handmade items, the ones they sold to the public, and often when the demand surpassed the supply they would sub-let work to their neighbors who were bound to do it according to Shaker standards.

Making the horsehair sieves was a tedious chore as the horsehair bottoms had to be woven in a loom, then they were bound on the edges and inserted between two circles of thin wood, one slightly large than the other. Any type of wood could be used for the bands as long as it would bend easily. Sieves will be found with bands of different varieties, including pine, ash, and poplar. The choicest of these horsehair sieves are the small ones, usually around three to four inches in diameter in either round or oblong shapes. The majority of these small ones were made to be used in doctor's offices to sift the various powdered herbs used in the medicine he dispensed. Some of the small sieves had covers for both sides, that is one for the top and the other for the bottom. This kept insects and rodents from trying to eat the left over herbs and thereby damaging the horsehair in the process.

Fanny Farmer is credited with standardizing measurements for everything related to food, from the food itself to the seasonings. Prior to that time, the amounts of ingredients were described variously as a "glassful" with no thought to the size of the glass and "a lump of butter the size of a walnut." Shortly after the Farmer cooking schools and her books appeared, manufacturers began making upright tin sifters with a wooden handle on one side and a crank with a wooden knob on the other. Not surprisingly they had standard measurements printed on the side.

Unusual wooden rolling pin with removable end. Reason unknown, but it makes an excellent place to hide money. $25-30.

Another sieve-like tool was the winnowing basket. It was necessary to separate the wheat from the chaff as well as the shells or husk from oats, rice, beans, or peas. These foods, whether to be used for seed for next year's planting, feeding the livestock, or for food for the family, were harvested and taken to the barn where they were spread to dry. Once dry they were beaten with a flail to separate the grain from the chaff. For those not familiar with a flail, it was a handmade device consisting of a long, wooden handle with a shorter piece fastened onto it, rather loosely, with a leather throng. Skill was required in using it because it had to be swung in such a way that the short piece would hit the grain hard enough to separate the grain from the chaff, yet not crush it. When this chore was finished, the remaining grain and husks that still adhered were placed in a large woven, winnowing sieve or basket and the contents tossed in the air until the husks were blown away.

Trays of all kinds were important to homemakers half a century ago because all china and silver usually had to be taken to the table as well as the food. In those days food was prepared in the kitchen, but it was always served in the dining room. The trays were indispensable for these chores as everything that had been brought to the table had to be returned to the kitchen after each meal. That explains why each family had several trays. They might have a picture or scene in the bottom, or they might have been one of the basketry types made by the women themselves.

One elderly lady told of spending an entire winter making a tray with a seed mosaic design. The maker gathered and dried all types of small seed pods, everything from wheat to milkweed. She also caught a few butterflies and prepared them. Once her tray base was made, she filled the bottom with her design, one that looked very natural with butterflies flitting among the wheat and small seed pods. Glass then covered the bottom. The tray itself could be made by the same person who made the bottom, or it could be made by the neighborhood basketmaker. Again it seems to have depended on the area in which it was made as reed and rattan could be ordered, therefore used anywhere, but the sweet grass was more or less native to the northeast while the long pine needles required for basketry are found in the south.

Then there is the tray one can individualize to make it their own. Look for an old wooden tray from the 1950s, one with a design and glass in the bottom. Remove the glass, insert a piece of your favorite needlework, replace the glass, and you not only preserve your needlework, but have a chance to show it off to an advantage.

Trivet collectors have to decide early just what type they want to collect. The hardest to find and the most expensive are the old ones dating back to the early 1800s. Then there are the later ones, some made of iron to look like the older ones, and some made with entirely new designs. There are also a number of aluminum trivets dating around 1950, maybe earlier. Some of them were painted black, probably to pass for iron. It is very easy to tell which material was used as aluminum is very light in weight. Another trivet that also dates from the 1950s is the electric example. Apparently it is not too desirable yet as they can be seen at flea markets and in antique malls priced in the $5 range.

Some of them are very attractive, and one found in the original box claims to be hand decorated, and probably was as much hand work was still being done at that time. According to the instructions found in the box, the electric trivet keeps coffee and casseroles at the right temperature — just ready to be served from the buffet or the table, they said. The decorated ones made ideal decorations when not in use. This particular one was made by Paragon Electric Company, Two Rivers, Wisconsin.

Rolling pins cover such a wide spectrum, a book would be required to include them all. There are collector who only want the rarest examples while other collectors want examples of every type made. That covers a lot of territory because they were hand made of wood with the entire rolling pin made of one piece, factory-made with attached, revolving handles, and manufactured in materials ranging from tin and aluminum, to stoneware and marble.

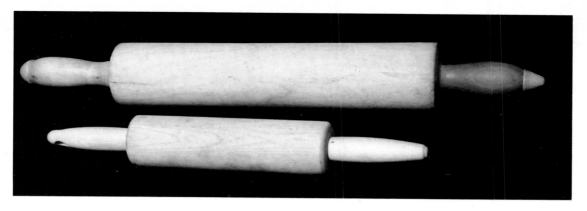

Two wooden rolling pins. Large $8-10, small $6-$9.

Three different wooden rolling pins, Middle had green handles, one made from single piece of wood. $10-$20 each.

Two aluminum rolling pins with red wood handles. $15-$20 each.

Wooden rolling pin for rolling cookie dough, other is porcelain with blue design. $20-$25 each.

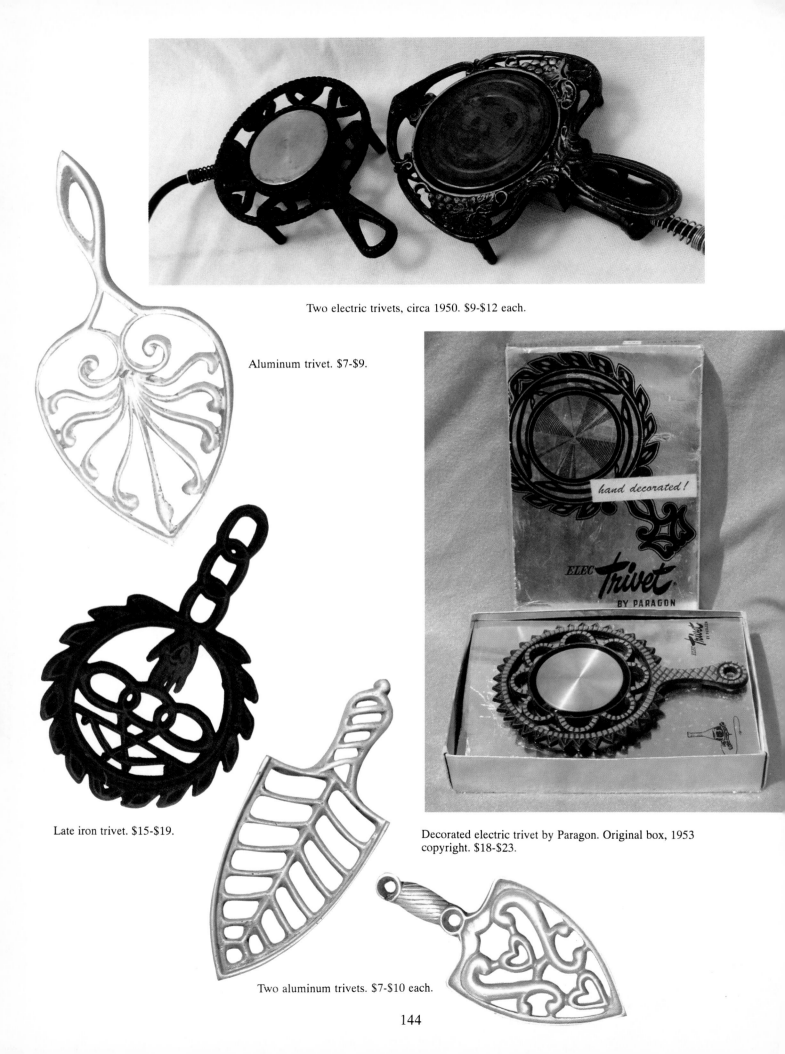

Two electric trivets, circa 1950. $9-$12 each.

Aluminum trivet. $7-$9.

Late iron trivet. $15-$19.

Decorated electric trivet by Paragon. Original box, 1953 copyright. $18-$23.

Two aluminum trivets. $7-$10 each.

144

Tray with painted paper design under glass. Metal border and handles.
$18-$24.

Large, oval seed mosiac tray with woven reed basketry border. $75-
$100.

Seed mosiac tray, dried seeds, leaves, and butterflies form a design on
the bottom of the tray. $40-$50.

145

Attractive trays can be made using 1950s wooden trays and adding a
favorite piece of needlework in the bottom. $20/25.

Woven reed tray with plywood bottom, painted design, a favorite in
the Fifties. $18-$14.

Small (5 by 7 inch) seed mosiac tray with sweetgrass border.
$24-$30.

146

Fancy silver plated tray. $20-$25.

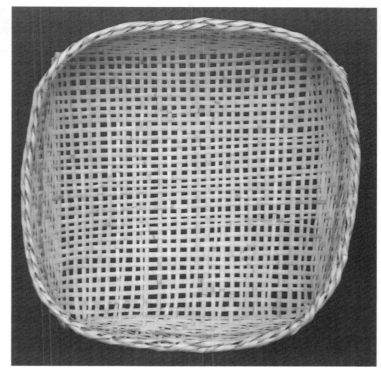

Large rivercane sifter. $45-$60.

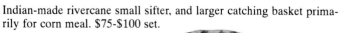

Sifter with fine cut splint woven bottom. $75-$100.

Sifter with horse hair bottom. $100-$125.

Indian-made rivercane small sifter, and larger catching basket primarily for corn meal. $75-$100 set.

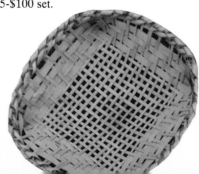

Sifter with rolled straw sides, both sides and bottom covered with cow hide. Homemade and rare. $100-$150.

Factory-made metal sifter for sifting flour. $9-$12.

Chapter Seventeen
Small Tools

Perhaps no kitchen tools or utensils have gained as much in popularity during the last decade as the small tools: the forks, the ladles, the cake turners, the can openers, the various spoons, the can and bottle openers, the soap savers, and especially the egg beaters. One of the reasons for this popularity is price. Nearly any of these small tools can be bought for under $10, many for $5 or even less, while the price of some larger tools and utensils can go as high as $100 or more. Freedom to decorate as one pleases is probably the answer. If the homemaker only has a few dollars in a piece or even a dozen pieces, she isn't inclined to let that stop her when she wants to change the kitchen decor. On the other hand, if she has several pieces that cost $100 or more, she feels she has to decorate around them, not discard them as she can the small tools. Another reason for their popularity is the multitude of things available. The homemaker or the collector can pick and cull to get something just a bit different from that of their neighbor. If nothing else, they can get a different colored handle. Some of the collectors are buying the small handled tools, all in the same color. One collector used peg boards on her kitchen wall and hung dozens of tools — all with red handles. To complete the decor she used as many red kitchen accessories as she could find. It made a bright and cheery kitchen, one in which it would be a pleasure to work.

Green seems to be the next favorite color to collect and the one with a wide variety of tools available. During the Fifties, Sixties and on into the Seventies this country went through a green phase, that is all appliances like stoves, refrigerators, and even the sinks were made of green materials. Bath-room fixtures were also made in colors including green. So it was only natural the tools and some of the utensils were also in green. They were in various shades of green and since then not only have some of the colors faded from much exposure to hot, soapy dishwater, but many have the enamel peeling off the handles. Thank goodness for the wide variety that is available. Collectors can pick and choose the best pieces at the best prices.

During the heyday of the inexpensive, small kitchen tools, these items could be bought at any 10 cent store like Newberry's, Kress, and Woolworth. Some hardware stores as well as some country stores had a generous supply of kitchen tools for sale. Large companies like Belknap Hardware and Manufacturing Company, Louisville, Kentucky offered the following kitchen tool and display deal in their 1937 catalogue: seven dozen kitchen tools plus a permanent display stand and price cards for $18.75. The tools consisted of a half dozen each of the following items: apple corer and parer, potato or fruit baller, single action egg beater, can opener, trowel-shaped cake turner, pierced blade cake turner, whipping spoon, batter whip, two tine kitchen fork, solid bowl ladle, potato masher, basting spoon, and mixing spoon. Everything in the deal sold for 10 cents each except the egg beaters that sold for 15 cents each retail. To pay for his display stand the merchant would have had to sell about fifteen dozen of these kitchen tools, but they did sell fast and the display would certainly be a permanent asset to his store, so he probably figured it was worth it. In those days merchants, especially those in the smaller stores, only expected to make a few pennies on each sale. The tools were described as having "the new hand fit stem green stain wood handles and black rust resisting ferrules.

Blue, yellow, and white handles as well as some in a natural wood finish were made, but judging by the number available now they certainly were not made in large numbers. In fact, there are collectors today who search for these scarce colors, and they admit they are hard to find.

Another small tool associated with both the kitchen and the bar is gaining in popularity, and that one is the cork screw.

Equally as popular in some circles is the bottle opener, and then there is the combination bottle opener and cork screw. Some of these were made in outstanding designs while others are perfectly plain — just a serviceable tool. One of the most expensive cork screws found in an old catalogue was the power worm type that sold for $6.30 a dozen wholesale in 1937. It was described as a worm type with cap lifter attachment. A power cup rested on the neck of the bottle and when the handle was turned the cork would rise into the cup which meant no pulling was necessary. The screw was made of tempered steel and was nickel plated. The wooden handle was enameled in green.

Many families still have gardens and the housewife still cans or freezes most of the excess food for use in the winter. It was ever thus. Many small tools were associated with this chore, and still are. Collectors not only buy them to decorate their kitchens, but also to use in canning season. Of course old glass, fruit jars are collectible, especially the beautiful blue and amber ones. But the small tools like the jar lifters that were used to lift the jars of fruits and vegetables from the canner are becoming popular, both for use and nostalgia. Then there are the can or fruit jar openers. The top had been sealed for several months when the housewife decided to open it. That was no easy chore so the manufacturers vied with each other to see who could make the best jar opener. Several examples are available now so the collector still has a chance to buy the one she likes best.

Half a century ago all farm wives made their own vegetable and fruit juices like grape and tomato. Once it was made, it had to be bottled. To get it into the sterilized bottles she needed a funnel. Again the manufacturers came to the rescue. They made funnels in many different sizes and as many materials. And this was where the bottle capper came in very handy. When the bottles were opened later, she needed a bottle opener. Everything had a purpose and it all meshed together to make life more pleasant.

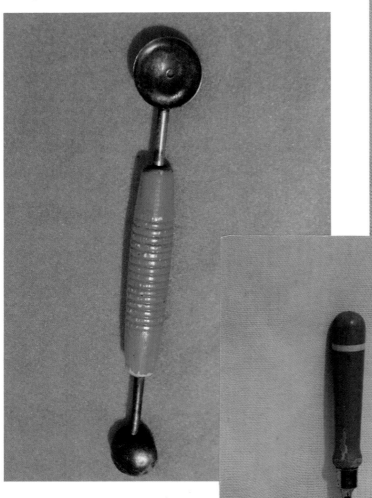

Green handled melon baller. $10-$12

Ladle with green handle. $6-$8

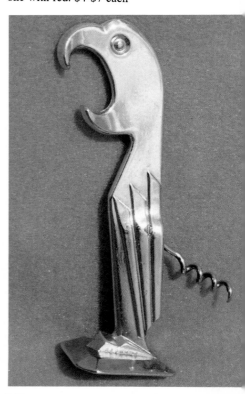

Two can openers, one with green handle, one with red. $4-$7 each

Different shaped bottle opener and corkscrew. $10-$15

150

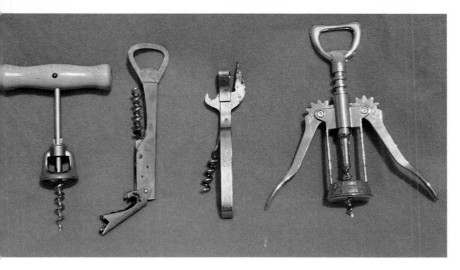

Four corkscrews. $5-$12 each

Small tin and aluminum funnels.
Old tin $7-$8, aluminum $3-$4

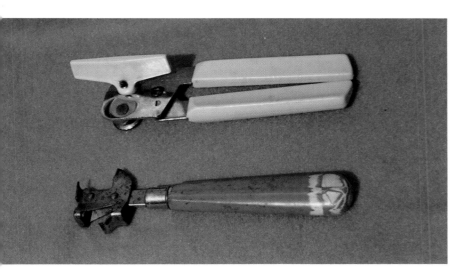

Two can openers. Green handle $8-$10, white $6-$7

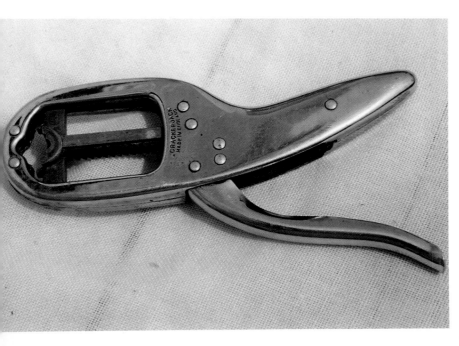

An argument arose at the mall where this was found. Some called it a
fruit jar opener, others a nut cracker. $10-$12

Gilhoolie fruit jar opener. $9-$11

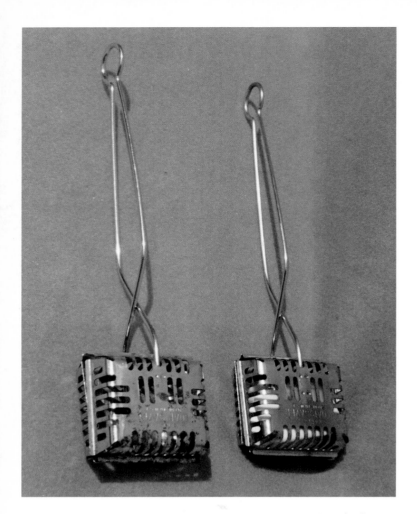

Late soap savers, scraps of soap were saved by putting them in the gadget then swishing it around in the water. $8-$14

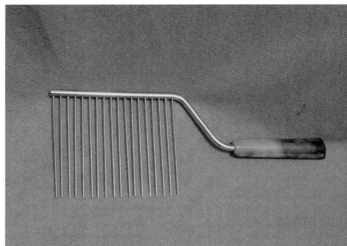

Cake cutter, Bakelite handle. $10-$12

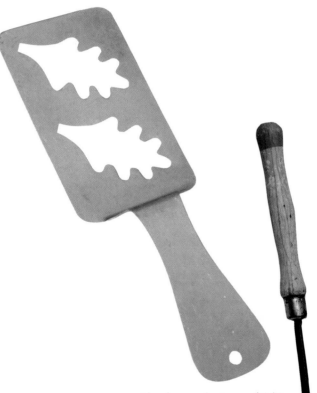

Aluminum cake turner. $6-$8

Meat fork, white handle with blue tip. $9-$11

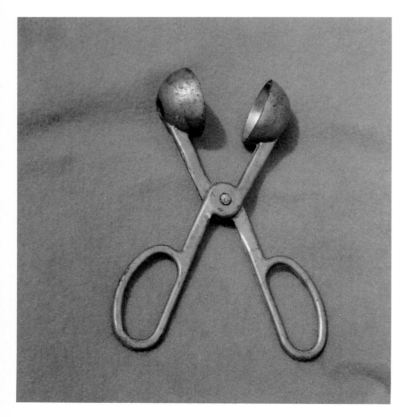

Swedish meat ball maker. $5-$6

Wooden salt and pepper shakers. $8-$11

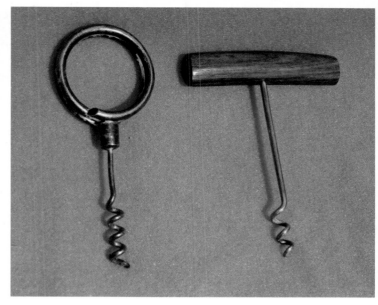

Plain corkscrews. $4-$6 each

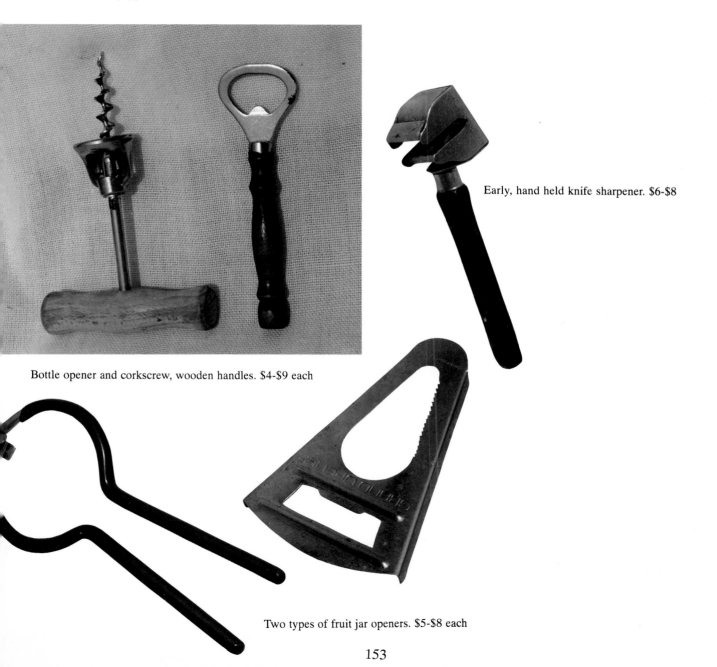

Bottle opener and corkscrew, wooden handles. $4-$9 each

Early, hand held knife sharpener. $6-$8

Two types of fruit jar openers. $5-$8 each

153

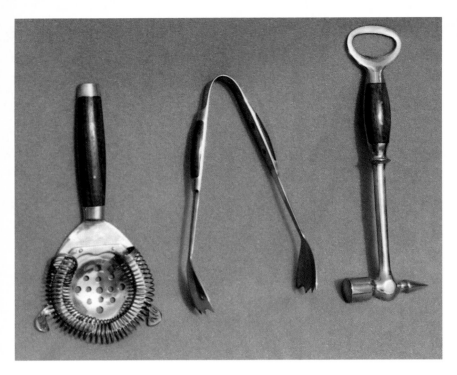

Bar tools were popular in the kitchen in the 1950s. Brass strainer, ice tongs, and bottle opener. $7-$9 each

Two small aluminum scoops. $6-$9 each

Early pot scrubber. $14-$17

Early handmade wooden soap dish or mold for lye soap. $28-$33

Three long handled, stainless steel spoons. $6-$9 each

Meat fork with hard-to-find yellow handle, knife with green handle. Fork $12-$15, knife $5-$7

Large ladle. $5-$7

Smaller ladle with deeper bowl. $6-$8

CLAM OPENER

Clam opener in original box. $8-$10

155

Chapter Eighteen
Tea Time

There is a tendency among many collectors, especially the older ones, to think of kitchen antiques as being a bit on the drab side, and chances are this all started with the wooden, tin, and iron tools and utensils used by the early settlers. Those early kitchens were drab indeed. But part of that stemmed from the lack of light as the windows were small and the panes were of poor quality glass. Combine that with the black iron, woodburning cook stove and the dark iron cooking utensils and you do get a drab image.

Things began looking up with the introduction of pewter tools and utensils the masses could afford. Then the bright and shiny tin began to be made and sold by the tinsmiths who toured the country selling and repairing their wares. Then manufacturers began making the brightly colored graniteware — well not at first because the first was gray, white, and mottled blue and white — which was a vast improvement over the iron and even the pewter and tin. Later there would be aluminum cookware which was not much brighter than the tin, but was heavier, and therefore more serviceable.

But we seldom think of cut glass, good china, and silverware as being part of the kitchen scene, and it really wasn't. Yet tea time, which referred to that afternoon repast, was a combination of the kitchen and the finest the homemaker had to offer. This was the one opportunity where the ladies had a chance to really show off their best linens, silver, and china without husbands or children. This was a woman-to-woman thing where they could show off their best cuisine, silverware, and linens. Most of the linens had been made by the hostess so it gave her a chance to hear the oohs and aahs of her friends. Of course there were times when the husbands and children joined them, but generally it was for ladies only.

To think this all began with that tiny, little tea leaf. It might be tiny, but it has been credited with the creation of more tea related items and events than probably any other single item. Maybe the following aren't in chronological order, but who among us can establish a correct date for the introduction of each? There can be little doubt the tea pot came first, to be followed immediately by the cup. Then came the tea biscuits, tea cozies, tea sets, tea services, tea tables, tea carts or wagons, and the tea cake, a sort of wafer-like cookie, all of which were made in enormous quantities and styles with the tea pots leading the list. So many were made in so many shapes, that they are one of the easiest thing to find today. In fact, tea pots were and still are so plentiful it is easy today to find a tea pot in any shape and nearly any price range the collector can afford. But tea inspired items and events didn't stop there; other examples include the tea party, tea dance, and the tea rose, a flower that is so pretty on the tea table.

To try to understand this fascination for tea it is necessary to go back as nearly as possible to the beginning. Of course that is next to impossible because so many legends abound, but one that seems fairly reliable tells of a Chinese emperor named Shen Nung who was so obsessed with cleanliness and purity that he boiled the water he drank. This occurred in 2737 B.C. which would make the emperor a leader in sanitation. One day as he was boiling his drinking water some leaves from one of the branches burning under his pot was caught up in a whirlwind, but they did not all blow away; some fell into his pot of boiling water. The aroma was so delightful, he decided to sample it. It tasted as good as it smelled, so the emperor began looking for leaves from that particular tree or shrub to make tea on a regular basis.

Other legends have been found concerning the origin of tea. Some say it originated in India or Japan, but the majority of people seem to believe the one about Shen Nung, maybe because it is such a simple story and it is easy to believe. None of the stories can be quoted as gospel as these legends were passed down from one generation to another by word of mouth. None can be substantiated with written facts. At that time there were not many people who could read and write. Most of them were men and they weren't that interested in the small leaves some person used to make a tea. They probably wondered if it would still be popular the next year.

Well, tea's popularity did last. By the Fourth and Fifth centuries, people were adding things to the tea to improve the flavor. Today we often add mint, lemon, or cream, but there was a time when it was suggested that cinnamon, onion, and orange be added to hot tea to improve the taste. It was also said that this drink "would render the drinker sober from intoxication and keep him awake." Tea was served hot for centuries, in fact iced tea is a real late bloomer.

One of the older and harder-to-find tea related antiques is the cup plate. Cup plates were not just for tea, but were used for coffee as well. The cup plate was a small glass disk used to hold the cup while the contents, tea or coffee, were poured into a saucer to cool. In those days it was the custom to drink one's tea as hot as possible. It was said that the hotter the tea, the better the taste, but from the pot to the mouth was such a short distance for near boiling tea they had to find a way to cool it, at least a little. The solution seemed to be saucering, that is the tea or coffee was poured into a deep saucer (all saucers were deep ones in those days) while the cup was placed on the cup plate.

By using the cup plate, a prettily patterned flint glass, it kept the hot cup from marring the table, or soiling the tablecloth in case some had spilled down the side of the cup.

Hammered aluminum cake stand, great for serving cake and cookies at tea time. Everlast trademark. $35-$45

Saucering one's tea resulted in the often used expression, "a dish of tea." Today society would probably frown on the custom of saucering one's tea, but in those day it was accepted as the correct thing to do. And why not? Everybody was doing it.

Another beautiful but hard-to-find tea related antique is the so-called night light tea pot. Why it was called a tea pot rather than a sick room light or maybe a toddy pot is unknown. It was given this name years ago and nobody has ever changed it.

The night light tea pot is believed to have originated in France where they called it a Veilleuse, but in America it became known as a night light. About a couple of centuries or so ago these exquisite china pieces were made by the best companies. Since some of them were made of the finest china and were used at night, it meant the user could stumble or drop them, and many were broken that way through the years. Of those left, many have found their way into private collections and museums. Once in a great while a collector will stumble onto one, but the chances of this happening are not good. Some later versions, however, can still be found. One of the most popular, the circa 1950 example with a Moss Rose design, is illustrated.

Both the old models and the later ones were found to be indispensable in the sick room. The light from the candle in the bottom was not strong enough to disturb the sick person, yet there was enough light for the nurse or the mother to watch the patient. The pot could be used to keep warm broth for the patient, keep water hot for medication, or to make a cup of hot tea. Or it could come in handy on a cold winter night in any room of the house where the occupants wanted hot water to make a toddy.

The tea table was usually round and medium-sized, the style and size that is much sought after today. Of course the demand for these tables has had an effect on prices; tea tables are very expensive now. The tea table was usually covered with a fine tablecloth that might be heavily embroidered, crocheted, or made of Battenberg lace. Whatever type of needlework had been used to make it, the tablecloth had to be elegant. This was the time when the hostess invited her peers, and what better time to show off her best needlework.

The napkins might be folded simply, or they might be in napkin rings. The sterling silver napkin rings that were so popular half a century ago have been replaced with simpler ones made of pewter, glass, or even aluminum. During the time the sterling napkin rings were being replaced, so were the fine china and cut glass. In fact, the tea table itself was being replaced with either wicker or some type of plain table on the veranda rather than in the sitting room or dining room.

Serving tea was no longer considered "entertaining," instead it was simply serving refreshments. Of course there were still a few of those gracious Victorian ladies who insisted on their afternoon tea, but they were fast dwindling in number. They continued to use the best silver, china, and linens, but in the newly built sub-divisions the modern homemaker was using less expensive china like Fiesta, Harlequin, and Riviera ware. In this environment where the tea table and the tea cart had never been used, refreshment were usually served in the kitchen or the dinette.

By the 1950s, the snack set had all but replaced the very socially accepted tea of another generation — at least the new homemakers seemed to prefer them. Albeit the snack set is said to have been around since sometime in the Twenties and Thirties, it does not seem to have reached its peak of popularity until the Fifties. This was the time when the majority of young war brides were establishing new homes, and since many of them were no longer working, they wanted to join the social scene. But for many the problem was a financial one — they just didn't have the home or the money to entertain as their mothers and grandmothers had. So, they settled for Home Demonstration shows and parties.

Usually one person in the new sub-division was selling something, anything from baskets to plastic cooking tools. She would persuade a neighbor or friend to have a party where she could demonstrate and sell her products. The hostess received a prize according to the number of sales made during the show. As we have said before, money was not all that plentiful so the demonstrator always advised the hostess to keep the refreshments simple, usually a slice of homemade cake and coffee.

The snack set was absolutely perfect for this kind of entertaining, and it made the simple little glass plate with the matching cup famous. Everybody had several sets. It became so famous, in fact, it was used at all types of club and church meetings, even those where a sandwich, a piece of cake or pie, and a cup of tea or coffee was served.

Everything that goes around, comes around, so they say. Therefore it is not unusual now to find those same snack sets being sold as collectibles — this time around. At first, they were only seen for sale at yard sales where they were priced around $1 for a set of four. Incidently, the early ones came in sets of four, or if the hostess thought she might need more and she usually did, she could buy several sets. Then they began showing up at flea markets, and recently they have been seen in antique shops and malls. Most were made of glass, but some nice china ones have been seen.

One of the tea related antiques and collectibles that we seem to treasure most is the tea pot. Regardless of the size, shape, or material we will buy it and give it a place of honor among the other things we collect. Perhaps the reason for that is it has been around so long and it has graced nearly every home, therefore we are more familiar with it. But with this obsession with tea pots we seldom see tea cozies, a covering for the tea pot that helps keep the contents hot.

One of the most interesting things we found in our tea research was the fact that despite the popularity of tea sets it was so easy for our ancestors to get free ones. Well, not exactly free, but without money. A little work was required instead. One example of this was the offer McCALL'S MAGAZINE made in 1899. They offered anyone a free 56 piece china tea set for selling 15 subscriptions to their magazine. This shouldn't have been a difficult job as the cost was only 50 cents for a one year subscription. And McCALL'S was not the only one offering tea sets for selling subscriptions. NEEDLECRAFT, the needlework magazine published in Augusta, Maine offered two similar sets. One set had a floral design with lots of orange color that reminded one of a beautiful sunset. The other set was predominately blue. These sets were smaller with only six cups and saucers, a creamer, sugar dish, and a tea pot.

Toothpicks are not put in holders on the table now like they were half a century ago. Although not used too frequently, the holders are still very collectible. Clear pattern glass $8-$10, late china $4-$5

Late pottery beverage set, attractive to use or for display. Circa 1980, $18-$23

Hammered aluminum bowl with divider, also excellent for serving. Everlast trademark. $30-$40

Cutwork napkins, pewter napkin rings. $16-$20 set of six napkins, $15-$17 set of six napkin rings

Early and late Blue Willow plates. Large $15-$18 in good condition, late $6-$8

Blue and yellow dinner plates, Riviera Ware.
$7-$9 each

Two blue Harlequin gravy boats, and green sugar. Gravy boats $15-$18 each, open sugar $5

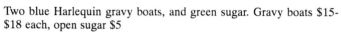

Four Riviera Ware breakfast plates in assorted colors. $5-$9 each

Riviera Ware salad and bread and butter plates in assorted colors. $5-$8 each

Metal tea caddy from England. $15-$25

Old Japanned tin tea caddy. $27-$35

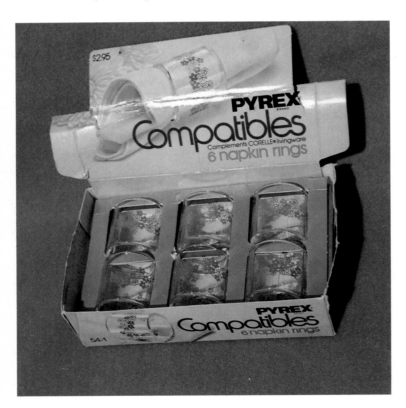

Six Pyrex napkin rings in original box, circa 1955. $20-$24

Caddy full of aluminum coasters. Unmarked. $3-$4 each

Silver plated tea strainer. $8-$10

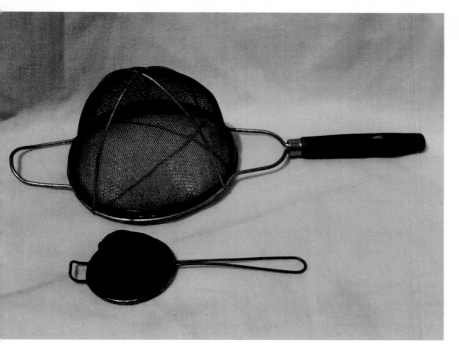

Two tea strainers, large for making pitchers of tea, small for cup. $6-$8 each

Amber Daisy and Button with Crossbar mugs were special favorites for serving children at tea time. $23-$27

Aluminum compote, great for serving candies, cookies, and cakes. Buelinum trademark. $26-$33

Small cut glass dishes were more at home on the sideboard or the dining room table, but were often moved to the tea table and filled with bon-bons during the heyday of tea time. $35-$45 each

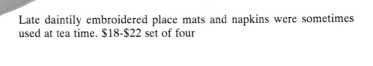

Late daintily embroidered place mats and napkins were sometimes used at tea time. $18-$22 set of four

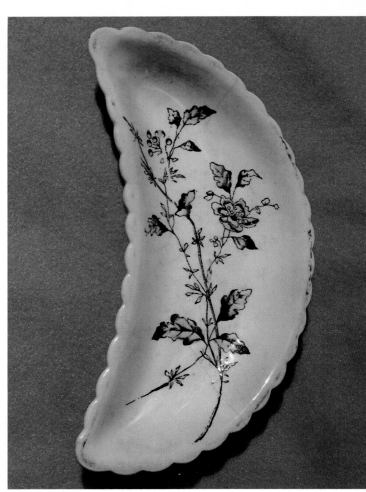

China bone dish. $12-$15

China bone dish. $11-$14

African-made mat, used to protect tea table from hot water or tea pots. $35-$40

Small Quimper bowl marked Henriot Quimper, France. $95-$120

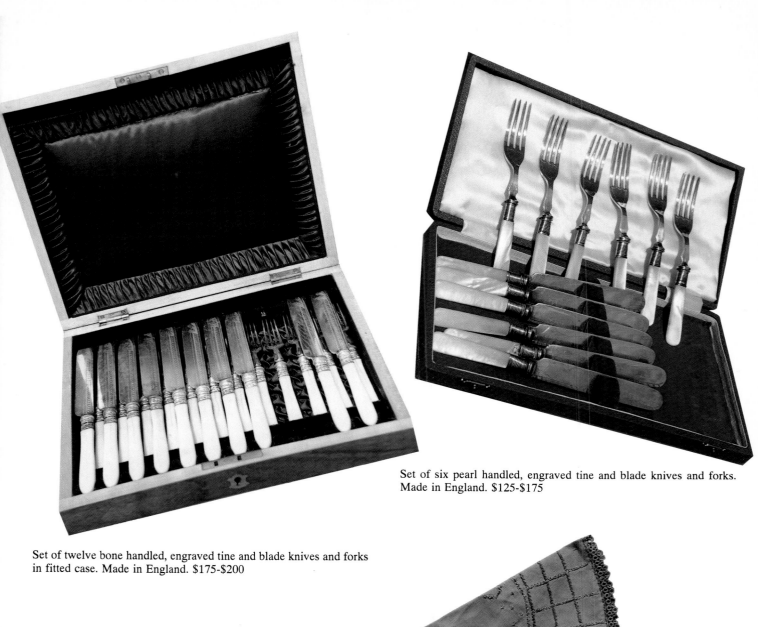

Set of six pearl handled, engraved tine and blade knives and forks. Made in England. $125-$175

Set of twelve bone handled, engraved tine and blade knives and forks in fitted case. Made in England. $175-$200

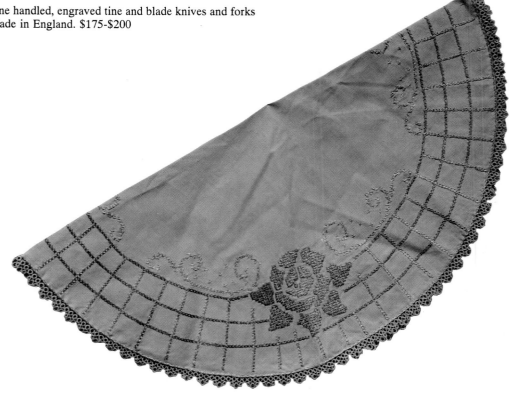

Round table cloth with tatted lace and silk embroidery, to fit a tea table. $20-$25

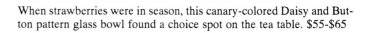

Filet crochet tea table cloth. $25-$35

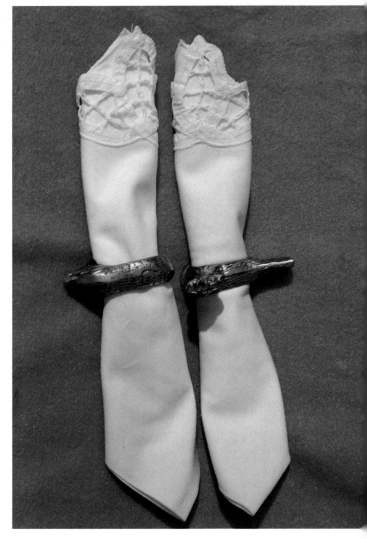

When strawberries were in season, this canary-colored Daisy and Button pattern glass bowl found a choice spot on the tea table. $55-$65

Napkins with Battenberg lace on one corner, pewter napkin rings. Napkins $14-$16 set of four

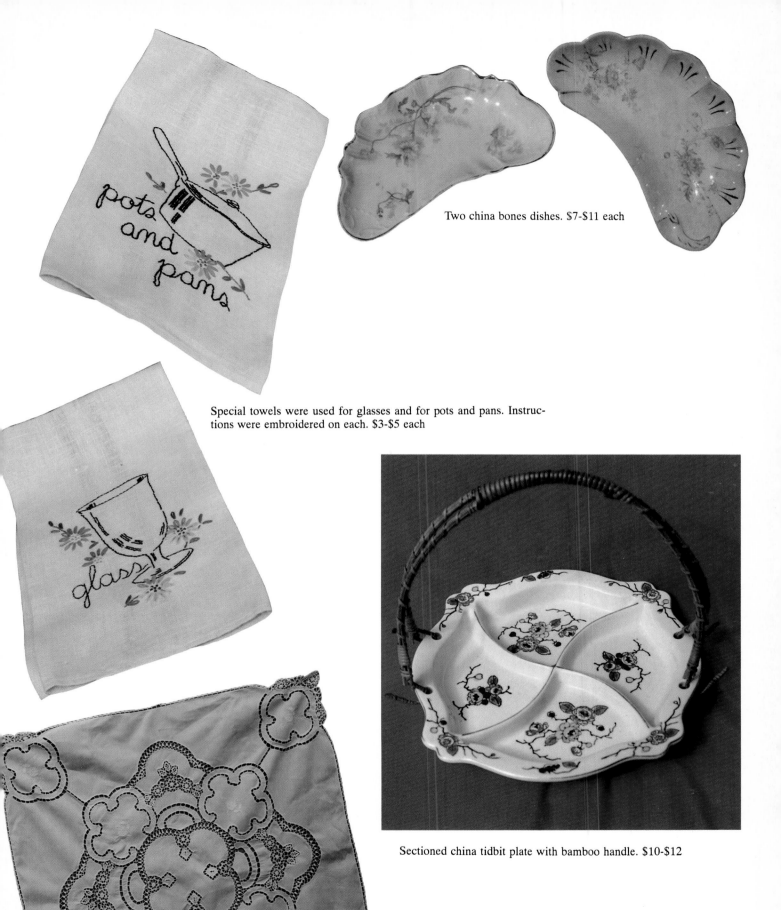

Two china bones dishes. $7-$11 each

Special towels were used for glasses and for pots and pans. Instructions were embroidered on each. $3-$5 each

Sectioned china tidbit plate with bamboo handle. $10-$12

Cut work table cloth for the tea table. Cut design is filled with crochet. $25-$30

China and glass butter pats were used on both the dining table and the tea table, but their popularity faded along with tea time. Very collectible now. China $3-$5 each, glass $6-$8 each

Cast aluminum tea pot with holder for loose tea leaves. Super Maid Cookware mark. $25-$35

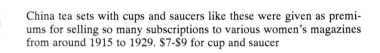

China tea sets with cups and saucers like these were given as premiums for selling so many subscriptions to various women's magazines from around 1915 to 1929. $7-$9 for cup and saucer

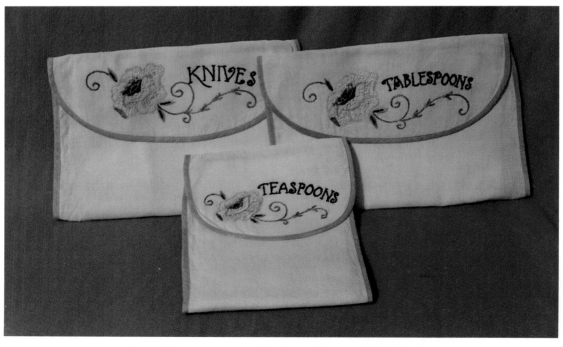

Loose flat ware was stored in flannel-lined, embroidered cases. $9-$11 each

Pyrex tea pot. $30-$35

Thin glass tea pot with glass holder for loose tea. Marked Saale-Geas, half liter. $30-$40

Gaily decorated cup and deep saucer. $75-$85

Pink Lustre, handless cup and deep saucer for saucering one's tea or coffee. $150-$200

167

Tea pot with tea ball attached to lid. Marked Universal Tea Ball Tea Pot, Landers, Frary, and Clark, New Britain, Connecticut. $75-$95

Same tea pot with lid off to show how tea ball is attached.

Small, late night light teapots were also handy for keeping a cup or two of tea hot. $15-$20

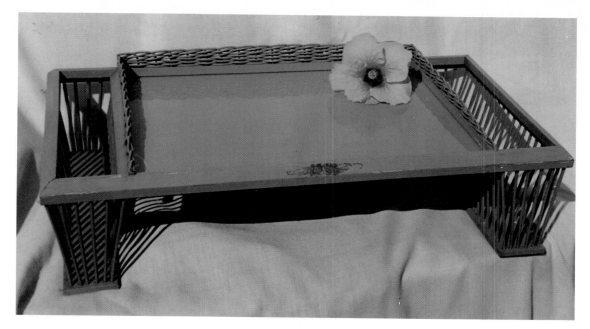

Breakfast trays were often used around the tea table for older family members or guests unable to manage their food without support. $25-$30

Ash splint and sweet grass, Indian-made, hot pad. $15-17

Electric tea pot marked Universal, patent dates from 1912 to 1924. $40-$45

Tea pot with matching stove, has fine mesh tea leaf holder. Both pieces marked Jos. Heinrichs, Paris and New York. $100-$150

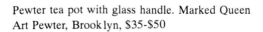

Showing Heinrichs pot and stove separately.

Pewter tea pot with glass handle. Marked Queen Art Pewter, Brooklyn, $35-$50

Plates like this one were very popular during the 1930s when tea time was still enjoyed. $15-$19

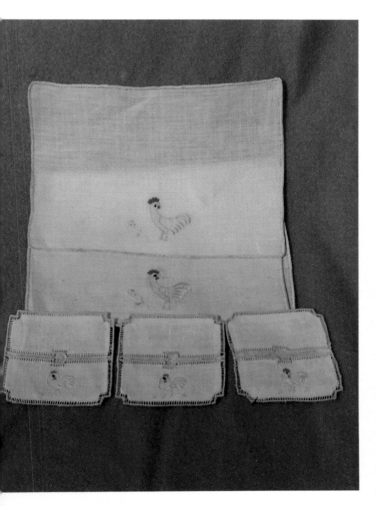

Two pattern glass toothpick holders. Blue one on left shaped like a top hat $27-$30, clear glass $10-$12

Embroidered coasters that slipped over the foot of the wine glass with matching cocktail napkins. $18-$23 set of four

Snack sets are late bloomers in the collectibles field. The single cup and plate from each pattern seems to be more sought after than complete sets — so far. $4-$7 one cup and plate

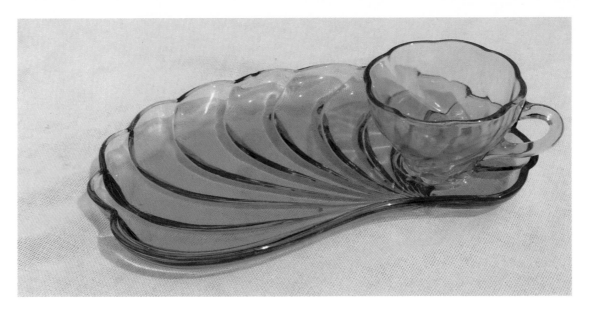

Blue Seashell pattern snack set. Colors scarce. $6-$8 each

Clear glass snack set with heavy grape design. $5-$8

China snack set with wheat design. $3-$5 each

Clear glass snack set, teardrop design in tray, fruit decorated cups. $5-$8

172

Chapter Nineteen
Waffle Irons, Hot Plates, and Fans

Waffles have been eaten in this country for about as long as some of the corn dishes. In the beginning there was not much to use with the corn dishes, but as soon as families acquired cows to supply the milk, a few chickens for eggs, and some flour — the basic ingredients — they began making waffles. And they have not stopped yet, although the majority now are bought frozen at the supermarket.

The ease with which waffles could be made and served contributed to their popularity. Almost from the beginning all the cook needed was milk, flour, and eggs along with long-handled waffle irons they could have made by the blacksmith. In the early days of waffle eating, food was cooked in or on hot coals from the fire in the fireplace. Waffles were no different. In fact, an 1839 recipe took the homemaker right through the process. First, the waffle irons had to be heated moderately, greased with fresh lard or butter, then filled with the waffle batter. The irons were closed, and the ring on the handle slid into place to hold the contents tightly. The filled irons were placed on a level bed of hot coals so both sides would cook evenly. If the cook was not experienced, she might have to open the irons and check whether or not the waffles were done. When done to a golden brown, they were stacked on a plate and served with lots of butter.

In addition to the butter, there were other toppings that varied from one region to another. It all depended on what the cook and her family had in the larder, and if they were fortunate enough to have a variety, it could depend on their taste. Generally in the northeast it was maple syrup while in the south cane syrup was the choice. In some areas they preferred molasses, while everyone loved honey on their waffles. Then there were always jellies and jams, the homemade varieties.

Another reason waffles have experienced such a long run of popularity lies in the many ways they can be changed, and changed so easily with the addition of another ingredient or two. One old recipe suggested using cream rather than "sweet milk" as the cream made the waffles much richer. Another suggestion involved the addition of "a little pounded cinnamon or lemon rind rasped with sugar" along with 2 ounces of pounded sugar and 2 ounces of clarified butter. This addition, they said, would change plain waffles into a gourmet dish. Other old recipes were found for rice waffles, Virginia waffles, raised waffles, and waffles served with boiled cider. The cider topping was made by boiling twice as much cider as sugar until the mixture reached the consistency of syrup. It was then poured over the waffles. This gave them an apple flavor.

From the early days onward, our ancestors had the basic ingredients to make waffles. They were a tasty dish, and one that was easily prepared, so they quickly became a favorite. They were not only served to the family but to guests as well. They could be served for any meal, but somehow in the scheme of things they ended up being a favorite for breakfast or the evening meal. Recipes did not recommend them for the noon meal, nor was any mention found of them being served at that time.

Although electrical waffle irons were made during the first decade of the twentieth century, they were not that popular simply because so few people had access to electricity. In the very early days, electricity was only available in the larger cities and then for only a few hours at night. It had been created to furnish lights at night and that served the purpose, the electric companies thought. Then it became available on Tuesday — just for ironing. But it became such a success when so many electrical appliances became available that electricity was turned on all day. As time passed, electricity became available to more cities and towns, but the small towns and villages along with the rural areas didn't get electrified until after World War II. When it finally became available to the masses it was hard to believe how many electrical appliances, including waffle irons, were sold. Proof of that was found in a copy of the January, 1949 CONSUMER REPORTS. They had not tested electrical waffle irons since 1939, and then they found that over eight million had been sold in that ten year period. That was a lot of waffle irons considering the times, the population, and the fact there were thousands of households still without electricity.

In 1939 electric waffle irons could be bought for as little as $10, but the coveted irons were those in a set that consisted of a waffle iron, a batter pitcher, and a tray for carrying it all to the table. This was a continuation of the cooking-at-the-table syndrome with the waffle iron being one of the leaders of the pack.

Manufacturer's names found on waffle irons include Arvin Lectric Cook, Berstead, Coleman, Dominion, General Electric, Hot Point, Knapp-Monarch, Kenmore (Sears), Manning Bowman, Montgomery Ward, Nelson, Sunbeam, Universal (Landers, Frary, & Clark), Westinghouse, and White Cross. Now and then waffle irons will be found without a nameplate. On the poorly made ones it can only be assumed they were made by a small company that did not have a name recognizable enough to be worth advertising; if, however, they are quality-made, the nameplate has probably been lost.

As soon as electricity became available there were thousands of inventors, some good, others wannabees, ready to make some appliance that would improve the lives of the people. In fact, nearly all the small electrical appliances were discovered within a couple of decades. It didn't take that much time to discover or invent them; it took time to sort the workable ones from the non-workable. Look at any patent records and there is no comparison between the number of inventions that were patented and the number that survived. Everybody thought they could build a better rat trap, and they all tried, but only a few examples were good enough to survive.

That appears to have been the case with the electric hot plate. In 1937 eleven hot plates were shown in one wholesale catalogue. There can be no doubt about the popularity of the hot plate. Some families might have as many as three or four, one for each food that was being cooked for the meal. Most farm women trusted their old woodburning cook stove; but were not yet convinced of the reliability of the electric cook stove so they chose to keep the old stove and buy hot plates for summer cooking. They wanted the heat from the woodburning stove in winter.

If we are to judge by the illustrations in the catalogues, the electric fan was more popular than the hot plate as there were illustrations for thirteen desk types and three floor models. There was also two ceiling fans, one with a light. Blade sizes ranged from 8 to 16 inches. Prices varied from $5.75 for the rigid 8 inch model to $62.50 for the oscillating 16 inch fan. The blades were made of Duraluminum, a material that was being used then to make airplane propellers. It was lighter and quieter than brass or steel, they said, and it would not rust or warp due to temperature changes. For a sign of the times, they stressed that the black blades were easier to keep clean and would not show dirt or fly specks.

Fancy one burner hot plate. $20-$27

Small, round hot plate. $18-$25

Early hot plate with screw-in plug on cord. $30-$35

174

Kenmore double burner hot plate. $24-$30

Fancy White Cross double burner hot plate. $35-$40

White enameled two burner hot plate. $23-$29

Early hot plate with cover. $30-$35

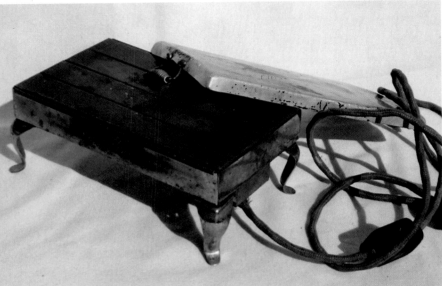

Same hot plate with cover removed.

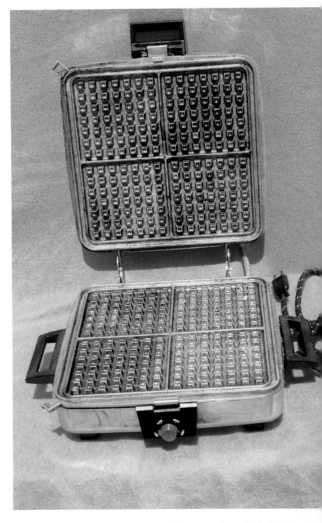

Single burner hot plate. $15-$19

Large waffle iron, makes four waffles at a time. $18-$23

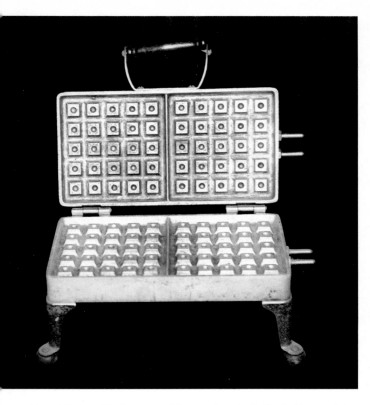

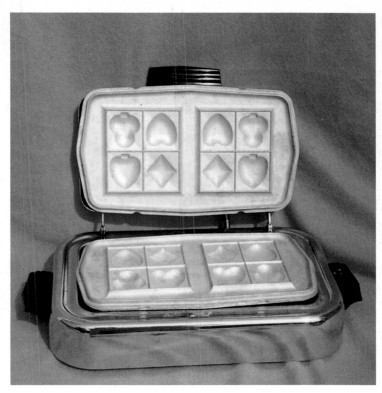

Circa 1925 waffle irons requiring cord on both the bottom and top. $23-$27

Aluminum plates for baking cookies in waffle irons. $14-$17

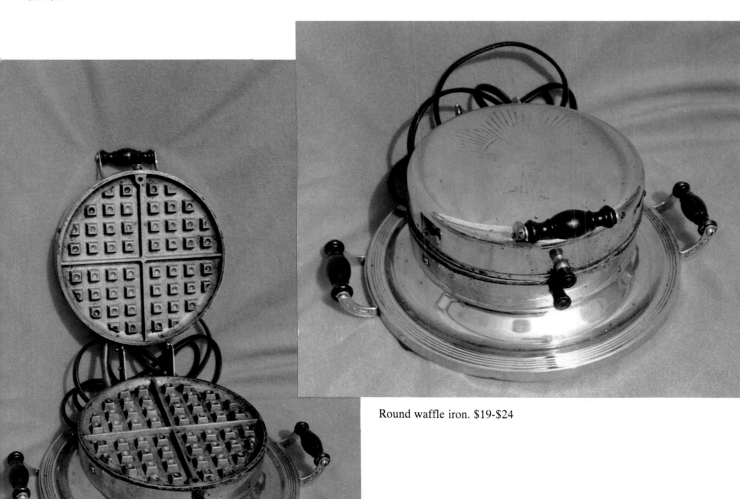

Round waffle iron. $19-$24

Same waffle iron open.

177

Round waffle iron with Bakelite handles. $25-$30

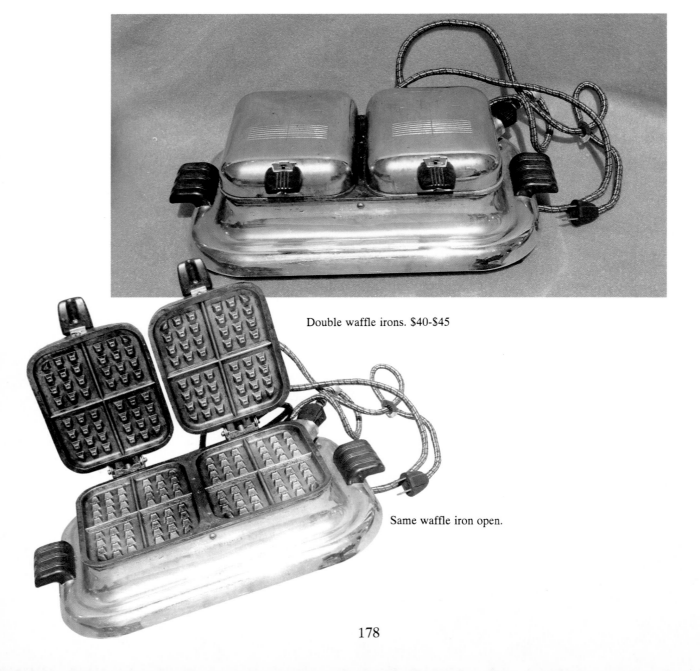

Double waffle irons. $40-$45

Same waffle iron open.

Waffle iron with wooden handles. $22-$26

Same iron but with grilling plates replacing the waffle plates.

Circa 1930 waffle irons. $17-$21

179

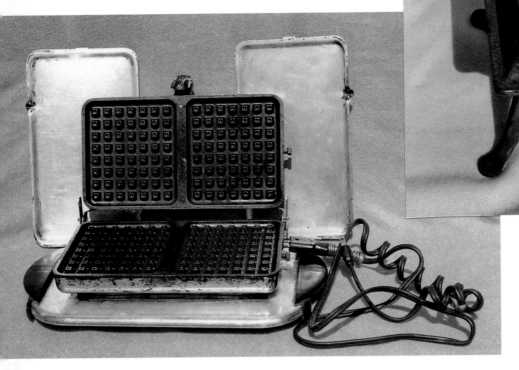

Waffle iron showing grill plates in back. On some waffle irons the waffle plates were simply turned over to form the grill. $35-$40

Early electric waffle irons. $50-$65

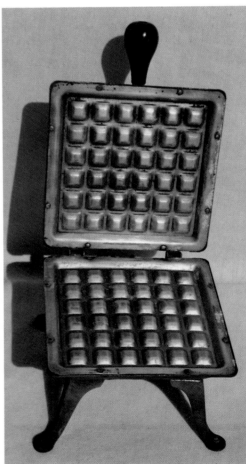

Same early waffle irons open.

Circa 1925 waffle irons open. $29-$35

Large Fostoria waffle irons. $29-$34

Waffle irons built on tray, temperature gauge built on top. $19-$26

Two Depression glass pitchers on tray. Large one for waffle batter, small one for syrup. Designed for making waffles at the table. Popular in Thirties and Forties. $45-$50

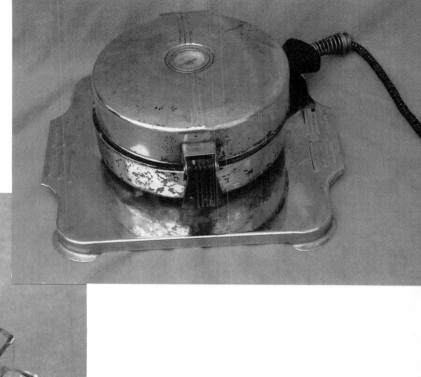

Aluminum covered plate kept waffles hot until they reached the table. $30-$35

Waffle server open.

Diehl electric fan. $23-$30

General Electric Whiz electric fan with brass blades. $125-$150

Super Air electric fan. $35-$45

Chapter Twenty
Wash on Monday

To fully understand what our ancestors endured on wash day so we can appreciate the wash day tools we now collect, it is necessary to go back to the early days when the dirty clothes were washed in the nearby lakes and streams, and rocks were used to beat out the dirt.

Monday has been designated wash day since the Pilgrim women went ashore on that eventful Monday in 1620 to wash some of the dirty clothes that had accumulated on the trip to the New World. That one act seemed to set a precedent that has survived until today — in some areas. For about three centuries Monday was religiously set aside as wash day. But Monday was not the only day designated for a certain chore. Those women had so much to do they had to work on a schedule. They always had lots of children who helped with the chores, but by the same token the more children they had, the more work they had to do. It was a never ending circle. Regardless of the size of the family, the wife and mother was expected to gather, prepare, and preserve enough food for the family. The father might bring in fish and game, but usually most of that had to be preserved for later use. She was also responsible for the family's clothing, admittedly not a lot for each person, but with a dozen children it still required a lot of fabric. That meant she had to gather the flax or the wool, prepare it, spin the yarn or thread, and then weave the fabric. None of these chores were exactly backbreaking, but when combined they presented a pretty full day.

Some women brought their old customs into America with them while others began adjusting to their new surroundings. Reports are women all adjusted, at least for years, to the following schedule: Wash on Monday, Iron on Tuesday, Bake on Wednesday, Brew on Thursday, Churn on Friday, Mend on Saturday, and go to Church on Sunday. Later they changed the schedule somewhat, apparently to better fit their needs. In the later version they replaced baking with mending and sewing. But during the next three centuries, the rules for three days never changed — wash on Monday, iron on Tuesday, and go to church on Sunday.

That leads us up to the time, not too long ago, when collectors seemed more interested in wash day tools than in their history. That was probably caused by the fact early collectors were closer to the time when the wash day tools were actually being used. Now there is a much younger group of collectors, many of whom don't remember anything about wash day beyond the automatic washing machine. They seem to be more interested in how the old tools were used, and writers, museums, and especially old farm restorations are fast becoming aware of this. More books are being written while the museums and restorations are sponsoring seminars and study sessions of various phases of farm life. Some are going so far as to actually have demonstrations on cooking meals in the fireplace, or on woodburning stoves.

As late as a century ago most families, unless they were the merchants or big plantation owners, didn't have too many clothes. Over the years many women quit weaving their own fabrics, yet they didn't have enough money to buy all the fabrics they needed. Since they had never had over two or three school dresses and one Sunday outfit, the children probably didn't notice. Worn clothing was used for work clothes while those the older children outgrew were passed on to the younger or smaller ones; therefore, the wash load remained the same, except when the family purchased or made new clothing and then the wash load grew. Combine that with the household linens, and it was a day long job.

Some of those early wash tools, especially the handmade ones, are the most intriguing. One example is the plunger type beater with the cutouts in the heavy base. The base was actually a portion of a limb or a small tree that was cut to size and to which a long handle was attached. No doubt the women thought this was a huge improvement over the old rock beating method. This plunger was used to help beat the dirt out of the clothes while they were boiling in the old iron wash pot. The clothing of the farm family could be badly soiled as the whole family worked in the dirt in those early days trying to clear the land as well as plant and harvest the crops. The tractor was a late bloomer, so most of the work done up until a half century ago had to be done with a mule and plow.

There was a time, not too long ago, when those old iron wash pots were much sought after. It is believed nostalgia created this collecting trend. Later they were used for planters after they had been painted, either black or white. They don't seem as plentiful now as they once were, nor has anybody been heard complaining. In their useful days the pots were not only used for boiling clothes, but for making hominy as well as lye soap.

Less than half a century ago women, especially farm women, were still making lye soap, a harsh soap that could be made very cheaply using a leach obtained from the ashes from the stove or fireplace. Some of the soap was usually taken out of the pot before the rest was boiled down to a hard soap. This so-called soft soap could be used as face or toilet soap and it was great for washing dishes. No written recipes could be found for making this soap as it was a sort of word of mouth deal passed from mother to daughter, but it was generally conceded that

Late tin washboard, painted blue. $6-$8

made of wood, tin, brass, glass, or graniteware. All of the old wash boards, the fancy ones, are quite scarce today, but later ones, those made during the 1940s and '50s are rather plentiful with reasonable prices.

Wash boards are still so popular, mostly for decorating purposes, that they continue to be made. Most of the new ones that have been seen are small in size, perfect for decorating, and can be painted various colors to match any decor, or they can be left natural — to age. The one illustrated is painted blue on one side and left natural on the other. The former owner used it in her keeping room, using the blue side for a while and then turning it over to help change the appearance of the room.

One of the more expensive wash day antiques is the clothes dryer that has fold up hangers. This device has three rows of hangers that can be pulled out to hold the laundry or which can be folded against the center post for storage. A second model, the accordion type, can be pushed together for storage or opened for use. Clothes dryers were, and still are, much more important in northern areas as the winters can be long and hard. It seldom gets too cold for too long in the south, the clothes can be hung out on the line year round. Only people without electric clothes dryers have a need for these, but lots of people keep them anyway, probably from habit.

Another wash day collectible that is as well known for other chores is the little one, two, or three burner stoves that was so popular in northern homes half a century ago. This small stove was very handy for boiling clothes on snowy days, or for just boiling a few pieces the family needed before the next wash day. It was also handy for cooking food, big meals or small, in the old copper ham boiler. It is best remembered today by women who were young girls half a century ago. They invariably describe it as the best heater they ever used for heating their hair curlers. In those days there were no electric curlers, only the kind with two handles that opened the curling iron.

If you like wash day antiques and collectibles, yet have limited display space in which to show off your collection, look for old clothes pins, the wooden push on type, or soap trade cards. The cards are rather plentiful and prices are still affordable.

three bushels of ashes and twelve pounds of grease would make half a barrel of soap. About the only time you will see or hear of lye soap today is at a craft or country fair where an older person has made some to sell to people who heard ancestors talking about it. In the waning days of soap making, the women resorted to using cans of lye purchased at the general store rather than go through all the work required to obtain the leach from ashes. The grease women used came from rendering the fat scraps at hog killing time and from used lard or fat they saved.

So many of the wash day tools were handmade it is sometimes difficult to determine exactly which was used first. Some might have been used earlier in one area while another was used elsewhere. A case in point is the plunger type washing tool and the so-called battling stick. The plunger type was used in the pot while the battling stick was used after the clothes were removed. A washing stick, a forked, wooden stick that was sometimes beautifully carved and other times painfully plain, was used to remove the laundry from the pot. The clothes were placed on the battling block which was actually a stump where they were beaten with the battling stick.

The battling stick lost much of its popularity when the wash board was introduced. By that time the country was in the middle of an industrial revolution, and it was no longer necessary for the father to make washing tools. Now the family could buy tin wash tubs to replace the old wooden ones, wash benches on which to put the tubs and the new fangled wringers so it was no longer necessary for the women to wring the clothes by hand. Then there were the very popular wash boards that might be

Trade card from Babbitt soap. $15-$19

Folding clothes dryer, newer models still in use for original purpose. Older ones sought after for same purpose and to use for displaying old linens at shows and malls. $15-$18

Late, unpainted tin washboard. $4-$7

Early tin washboard with vertical tin across the top. $15-$21

Old clothes line holder or winder, often used now for fishing lines. $35-$45

185

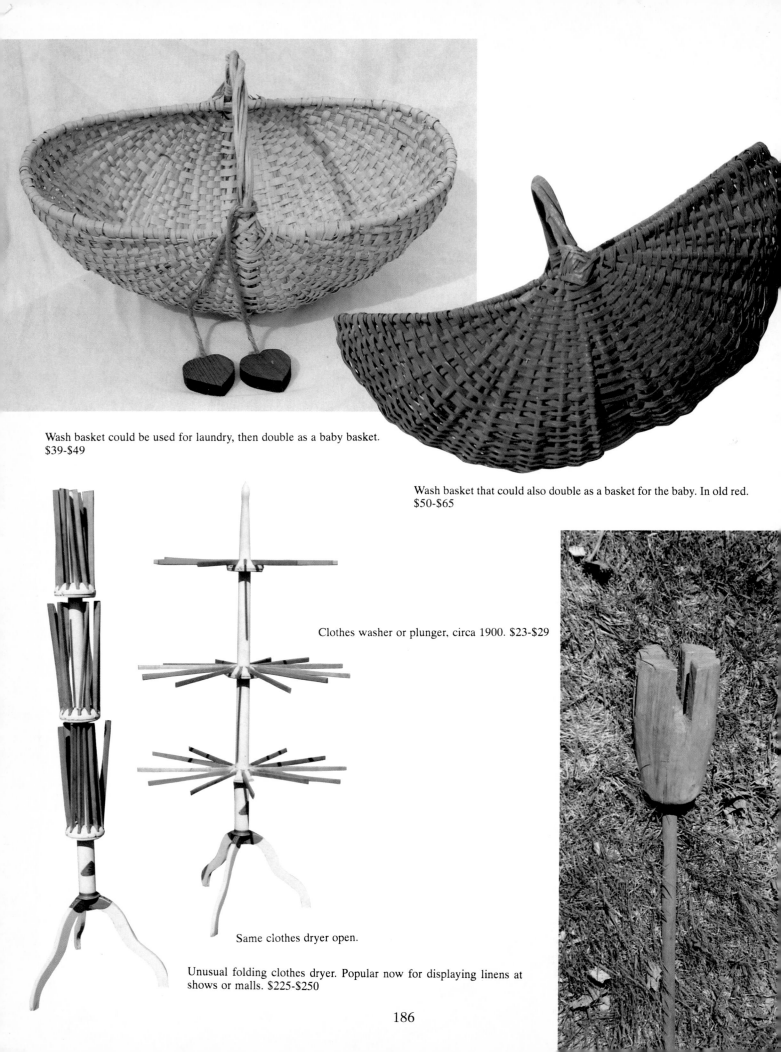

Wash basket could be used for laundry, then double as a baby basket.
$39-$49

Wash basket that could also double as a basket for the baby. In old red.
$50-$65

Clothes washer or plunger, circa 1900. $23-$29

Same clothes dryer open.

Unusual folding clothes dryer. Popular now for displaying linens at shows or malls. $225-$250

186

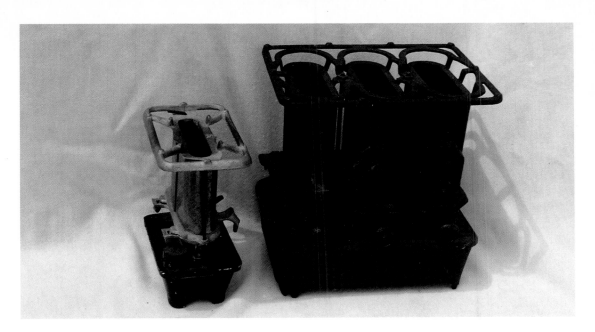

One burner and a three burner stove used for cooking, heating wash water and boiling clothes in winter, and heating the girl's hair curlers. Small $24-$30, large $40-$45

Two burner stove, Union brand. $30-$37

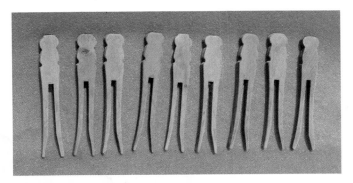

Wooden clothes pin from the 1930s, '40s, and '50s. $3-$5 a dozen

Chapter Twenty One
Woodenware

There was a time when people's lives actually depended on the fireplace. It was used to cook their food (there was no other way except maybe a campfire outside), and it was used to keep them from freezing in winter. This meant the kitchen was the family gathering place, especially at night. In this warm cozy atmosphere the "womenfolk" spun, wove, and did their mending while the men folk repaired farm tools and whittled or carved things needed for the house.

Perhaps the most important of those things were bellows as they were essential for keeping the fire going. They were used to fan the coals into a flame, provided there was enough fire left in them. In those early days, families treasured their bellows because when the fire was too far gone to be re-kindled, they had to send one of the children to a neighbor's house to borrow live coals. Since they cooked their food on the fireplace, they had to keep the fire going year round.

After the woodburning stove was introduced, the family kept several bellows. They were needed to keep the fires going in each of the bedrooms. One household might have up to a dozen bellows which explains why so many are available today. The men who loved to whittle never stopped and they made bellows until they died, which explains why there are still so many available — albeit late but beautiful examples that can still be found today. Living in what can only be described as a throw away society today, a society brimming with material goods, we have problems trying to understand how difficult it was for earlier generations to obtain even the simplest tool. Something as simple as a wooden spoon. In the majority of cases, that tool was whittled out at night while the family was gathered around the fire.

Those ever important bellows were generally made in three shapes: round, rectangular, and heart-shaped with the latter being the most popular. Three materials — wood, leather, and brass for the stems — were used on each.

Some of the most beautiful bellows have carvings on the wooden fronts, and Samuel McIntire, a noted Salem, Massachusetts wood carver is credited with being the first to carve bellows in this country. We tend to think of bellows as being a rather mundane, household tool that was necessary, but never outstanding. They might not have been as outstanding as other things, but bellows were very necessary. And that explains why so many patents were issued. Apparently it was a case much like the rat trap with each man thinking he could build a better bellows. As far as is known none were considered better than those made previously, but some had more interesting shapes and designs. The earliest date for a bellows patent is believed to be 1811 when a New Yorker named Charles McMurty received one. Shortly thereafter two men, Eckstein and Richardson, who lived in Philadelphia, applied for and received a patent for bellows. A South Carolinian named Forward as well as several New Englanders also received patents for their bellows designs. No record could be found on the type or design. Nor could any information be found on the manufacture, that is, where any of them were ever made.

Like so many things made, especially during the last century, there were many variations, both in the design and in the decorations. There were many whittlers and carvers working during the nineteenth century as well as many artists, some talented, some not so talented. But like the whittlers, they were looking for ways to use their talents; therefore, it isn't too surprising today to find a number of bellows with scenes painted on them. Even more surprising is the fact that the painted ones never seem to be priced as high as the carved ones. Maybe we have just been programmed to think the carved ones are better.

Again like any handmade item, the design varied with the maker, either the carver or the artist. Generally they seem to prefer flowers and animals, things that were familiar to them, Flowers seem to be a favorite with roses leading the list. Some of the bellows, especially those made later, have scenes carved on them.

The illustrated bellows has a lighthouse on it which makes one think it was made somewhere on the coast of Maine. It was found in Maine, which would add credence to that theory. But there is a chance it came from nearby Canada where they have been and still are creating carvings as outstanding as those done in Maine. It is impossible to date this one, although we know it is late. It could have been made for the tourist trade or it could have been made in the 1970s when the oil crunch forced many families back to using the fireplace. Then there is the wooden bellows covered with thin leather or a good quality vinyl. There is a possibility an old but damaged bellows has been covered to make it into a decorative piece.

Bellows were only one of the wooden things made by the husbands and fathers of the early families, and not only the early settlers as some men are still whittling and carving things needed around the house as well as a few decorative things like whales and birds to sell in gift shops. One item that is closely associated with kitchen collectibles in New England is the spruce gum box. Spruce gum boxes may be plain or quite elaborate, but they are all homemade and were made for the children to store their spruce gum. A half a century ago children did not have much money to buy packaged chewing gum, but if their fathers and brothers worked in the woods of New England they could always expect to receive pieces of spruce gum when the fathers found a spruce tree. Even if the gum did come free from trees, the children did not waste it. They kept the new in a spruce gum box while they chewed the old over and over. Today spruce gum boxes are not only scarce, they are also very expensive.

Bellows and boxes were not the only things made by the whittlers. They also made plain things like wooden spoons, knife boxes, and cutting boards. But perhaps the one thing they made where they could let their imagination run wild was the whirligig. In this case it was something that was both interesting and helpful. It was interesting because it showed the creativity of the maker and it helped to predict the weather — at least it showed the direction of the wind. And in those days when there was little or no weather reporting, the family had to depend on one of the older members of the family, one who had experienced many hurricanes (often called east gales by some) and tornadoes to try to predict the weather. The planting and harvesting of the crops depended greatly on the expected weather. For example, the family's entire yearly income depended on getting the cotton, peanut, or tobacco crop harvested and to market before the hurricanes arrived. By knowing the direction of the wind for several days, the experienced could predict the coming storms.

Early knife box in old blue paint. Used to sharpen knives. $95-$115

Holder for splinters or small slivers of wood to be used for starting a fire, usually in the fireplace. $50-$75

Handmade box for storing spruce gum. $75-$95

Homemade wooden spoon. $12-$14

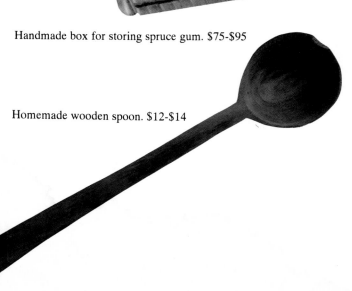

189

Wooden ladle probably used for stirring apple butter or similar food in small pot on the stove. $15-$18

One of those hard to identify handmade tools. Each person made tools to fit their own needs, and they also made them according to their ability which, at times, left much to be desired. This one could have been used to cut corn stalks for feeding the farm animals. $60-$75 for its uniqueness.

Late apple press. $20-$25

Two early wooden spoons. $10-$12 each

190

Late wooden bellows covered with leather. $25-$30

Late cranberry scoop. $10-$15

Monkey Pod wood cutting board or cheese board. $15-$18

Slotted wooden spoon. $9-$12

Two wooden spoons. Large one described as a candy spoon. $13-$17 each

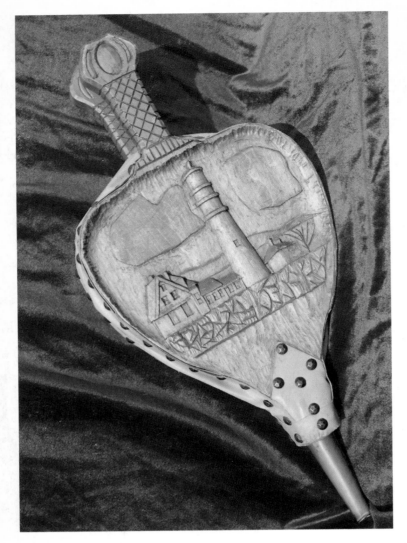

As the wind turns the wheel on this whirligig, the whale swims away from the lighthouse. $95-$125

Late carved bellows, may have been made in Canada. $50-$60

Handmade whirligig, red-headed woodpecker pecking on a tree. $100-$150

Wooden mold. $24-$26

Handmade wooden cutting board. $25-$30